READING COMPREHENSION WORKSHOP

PERSPECTIVE

P9-ANZ-157

GLOBE FEARON
EDUCATIONAL PUBLISHER

PARAMUS, NEW JERSEY

Paramount Publishing

Executive Editor: Virginia Seeley
Senior Editor: Bernice Golden
Editor: Lynn W. Kloss
Editorial Assistant: Roger Weisman
Product Development: Brown Publishing Network; Book Production Systems
Art Director: Nancy Sharkey
Production Manager: Penny Gibson
Production Editors: Nicole Cypher, Eric Dawson
Marketing Manager: Sandra Hutchison
Photo Research: Jenifer Hixson
Electronic Page Production: Siren Design
Cover Design: Carol Anson
Cover Illustration: Jennifer Bolten

Globe Fearon Educational Publisher wishes to thank the following copyright owners for permission to reproduce copyrighted selections in this book: **Dell Books, a division of Bantam Doubleday Dell Publishing Group, Inc.**, for Bette Greene, "An Ordinary Woman" from *Sixteen Short Stories* edited by Donald R. Gallo. Copyright (c) 1984 by Bette Greene. **Crown Publishers Inc.**, for Dave Barry "Shark Treatment" from *Dave Barry's Greatest Hits*. Copyright (c) 1988 by Dave Barry. **Don Congdon Associates, Inc.**, for Richard Matheson "Lemmings." Copyright (c) 1957, renewed 1985 by Richard Matheson. **The Fox Chase Agency, Inc.**, for Dave Barry "Shark Treatment" from *Dave Barry's Greatest Hits*. Copyright (c) 1988 by Dave Barry. **Richard W. Hill, Sr.**, for Rick Hill "Preserving Native American Culture Should Be a National Concern." **Alfred A. Knopf, Inc.**, for Piri Thomas "Amigo Brothers" from *Stories from el Barrio*. Copyright (c) 1978 by Piri Thomas. **Francis E. Izzo**, for Francis E. Izzo "Tank" from *Tales from Isaac Asimov's Science Fiction Magazine*. Copyright (c) 1979 David Publications.

Globe Fearon Educational Publisher wishes to thank the following copyright owners for permission to reproduce illustrations and photographs in this book: **p. 9**: Illustration by Dan Krovatin; **p. 16**: Illustration by Siren Design; **p.29**: Illustration by David Tamura; **p. 34**: Illustration by Kenneth Spengler; **p. 67**: Photograph, The Picture Cube; **P. 87**: Photograph courtesy of UPI/Bettmann Agency; **p. 113**: Illustration by Mary Lempa; **p.128**: Photograph, copyright by Snyderman, Southern Stock Photo Agengy; **p. 131**: Photograph, San Antonio Light Collection.

Copyright © 1995 by Globe Fearon Educational Publisher, a division of Paramount Publishing, 240 Frisch Court, Paramus, New Jersey 07652. All rights reserved. No part of this book may be reproduced or transmitted in any form or by any means, electrical or mechanical, including photocopying, recording, or by any information storage and retrieval system without permission in writing from the publisher.

Printed in the United States of America   5 6 7 8 9 10 99

ISBN: 0-835-90570-5

GLOBE FEARON
EDUCATIONAL PUBLISHER
PARAMUS, NEW JERSEY

Paramount Publishing

Contents

Unit ONE

BECOMING AN ACTIVE READER

Reading **short stories** actively means becoming involved with the characters. Have you ever found yourself joining in story conversations, judging characters' actions, or giving characters advice? Good readers often feel like a character's best friend.

Using Skills and Strategies

Asking questions about a short story's **point of view** can help you become an active reader. You might look back at a short story and ask: Who is telling this story? How does this point of view affect what I learned about the story's characters and events?

Noticing **multiple meaning words** is another way to become involved in a story. If the meaning you know for a word doesn't make sense in a sentence, you might ask: Do other words near this word provide clues to its meaning? Active readers check all of a word's meanings in a dictionary to find the one that makes sense in the sentence.

In this unit, identifying **point of view** and **multiple meaning words** will help you become a more active reader.

The Short Story: The Writer's Voice

Characters in realistic stories often look and sound like people we have met. Even when these characters have different backgrounds, their problems and how they solve them can be similar to situations we know. You can learn about the experiences of many different people by reading realistic stories. You can also gain insight into ways to deal with your own everyday problems.

Responding to Short Stories

Active readers know that the point of view of a story and the words that the author uses will affect their responses. In this unit, write your responses to the stories "Amigo Brothers" and "An Ordinary Woman" in the margins. You can use your notes to discuss the stories with classmates.

Point of View

| Lesson 1 | Introducing page 2 | Practicing page 3 | Applying page 4 | Reviewing page 17 | Testing page 18 |

Introducing Strategies

Authors write stories from different **points of view.**
Sometimes, authors use a first-person narrator—a main
character describing events, using *I* and *me.* Other times,
authors use a third-person narrator—an outside storyteller
describing events, using *he, she,* and *they.* In a first-person
story, the main characters usually focus on their own
thoughts and feelings. In a third-person story, the thoughts
and feelings of many characters may be revealed.

The diagram below shows how good readers identify and
respond to point of view while reading.

Identify	Look Back	Respond
Who's telling the story? Which words tell me this?	Can I find thoughts and feelings expressed by the main character? OR Can I find story events described by an outside narrator?	How did the point of view affect my response to the story?

Reading Short Stories

**Read the excerpt from the short story "Amigo Brothers"
on pages 8-11 and the sidenotes on page 8. These
notes show how one good reader responded to point of
view while reading. After reading, answer the questions
below.**

1. How does the reader know this story is written in the
third-person point of view?

_____

_____

2. How was the reader affected by this point of view?

_____

_____

Practicing **Point of View**

A. Circle the letter of the choice that best completes each sentence below. Then, on the lines provided, explain why you selected that answer.

1. In the third-person point of view, the narrator
   a. presents the story from one boy's viewpoint.
   b. describes the thoughts and feelings of both boys.
   c. stays out of the story.
   d. both b and c above.

_____

_____

2. If the author had used the first-person point of view, the narrator
   a. might not have revealed what both boys looked like.
   b. might not have described the feelings of both boys.
   c. both a and b.
   d. neither a nor b.

_____

_____

3. In this story, the third-person point of view helps the reader feel like
   a. a close friend to one of the boys.
   b. an understanding outsider who gets to know both boys.
   c. an intruder who is "spying" on the boys.
   d. a spectator who is far removed from the story.

_____

_____

B. Write a paragraph about two friends who are both facing the same challenge. Use either the first-person or the third-person point of view.

_____

_____

_____

_____

_____

_____

Applying *Point of View*

The paragraphs below are from the short story "The Fifty-Yard Dash" by William Saroyan. Read the paragraphs and think about the point of view the author uses. Then answer the questions that follow.

". . . It seemed to me that never before had any living man moved so swiftly. Within myself I ran the fifty yards fifty times before I so much as opened my eyes to find out how far back I had left the other runners. I was very much amazed at what I saw.

Three boys were four yards ahead of me and going away.

It was incredible. It was unbelievable, but it was obviously the truth. There ought to be some mistake, but there wasn't. There they were, ahead of me, going away."

1. Are these paragraphs written in the first-person or the third-person point of view? List some words from the paragraphs that helped you decide.

_____

_____

_____

_____

2. How did the point of view help you learn about the main character in the paragraphs? List some details from the paragraphs.

_____

_____

_____

_____

3. How did the point of view limit what you could learn about other characters?

_____

_____

_____

_____

_____

To review
⬇
page
17

Multiple Meaning Words

| *Lesson 2* | **Introducing** page 5 | **Practicing** page 6 | **Applying** page 7 | **Reviewing** page 19 | **Testing** page 20 |

Introducing Strategies

Authors often use **multiple meaning words**—or words with more than one meaning, such as *charge, watch,* or *check.* There is no way of knowing what these words mean when they are used alone. To figure out the meaning of a multiple meaning word, good readers look at how it is used in the sentence. If additional clues are necessary, readers look up the meaning of the word in a dictionary.

The diagram below shows steps readers can take to find the correct meaning of a multiple meaning word.

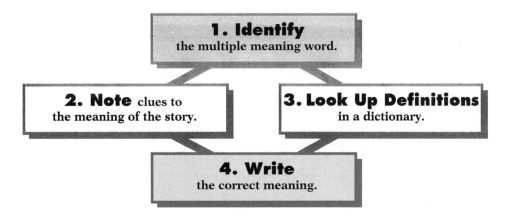

1. Identify the multiple meaning word.

2. Note clues to the meaning of the story.

3. Look Up Definitions in a dictionary.

4. Write the correct meaning.

Reading Short Stories

Reread the excerpt from "Amigo Brothers" on pages 8-11. As you read, circle examples of multiple meaning words. Then choose one word and answer the questions below. If necessary, use a dictionary to help you.

1. What word did you choose? What are some of its meanings?

_____

_____

2. What story clues can help a reader decide on the correct meaning? What is that meaning?

_____

_____

Practicing *Multiple Meaning Words*

A. The sentences below are about the story "Amigo Brothers." Look at the word in bold type in each sentence. Look up the word in a dictionary. Circle the letter of the definition that gives the best meaning of the word as it is used in the sentence. Then on the lines provided, tell why you chose that meaning.

1. To **spare** Felix hurt, he would have to knock him out, early and quick.
   a. stop from harming
   b. more than what is needed
   c. an extra
   d. score in bowling

   _____

   _____

2. The winner will represent the Boys Club in the tournament of champions, the Golden Gloves. There will be no **draw.**
   a. pull in one direction
   b. undecided contest; a tie
   c. take cards from a stack
   d. a football play

   _____

   _____

3. Antonio, hurt, sent back a blurring **barrage** of lefts and rights that only meant pain to Felix . . .
   a. artificial dam   c. rapid, repeated actions
   b. heavy artillery fire   d. outpouring of speech

   _____

   _____

B. Write a brief description of an exciting sporting event you attended or watched on television. Use at least three multiple meaning words in your description.

   _____

   _____

   _____

   _____

   _____

Applying *Multiple Meaning Words*

Read each example below and think about how the word in bold type is used. On the lines below each paragraph, write the correct meaning of the word. Use a dictionary to help you. Then circle the clues in the example that helped you identify the best meaning.

1. Whenever I acted loud and silly, my older brother told me not to joke around so much. He said that no one likes people who **exhibit** such annoying behavior.

_____

_____

_____

2. The girl quit the neighborhood club when she noticed that she was being used by the other members. She didn't like being the **pawn** of people who said they were her friends.

_____

_____

_____

3. The roof garden on top of the old apartment house had not been tended to for years. **Rank** weeds had overtaken the rose bushes, and there was little room for any flowers to grow.

_____

_____

_____

4. The rowers positioned themselves behind each other in the **shell.** We watched from the dock as they rowed together in unison.

_____

_____

_____

5. The new clerk at the corner deli was in **charge** of posting the luncheon specials.

_____

_____

To review

page 19

Piri Thomas (1928-) grew up in New York City in a neighborhood known as Spanish Harlem. He became involved with gangs and drugs and served seven years in prison. When he returned to his neighborhood, it was as a youth worker. His stories are intended to help young people deal with difficult times in healthy ways. This story comes from his collection titled *Stories from El Barrio*.

from **Amigo Brothers**

by Piri Thomas

The notes in the margin show how one reader thought about point of view while reading.

The words *they* and *themselves* tell me that the story is being told in the third-person point of view.

In this paragraph, the narrator describes what the boys look like. It's as if the narrator were standing outside the story, telling me what he or she sees.

The narrator is telling me about the boys' hopes and dreams. But this point of view makes me feel like an outsider.

Write your own sidenotes as you read the rest of the story. In your notes, focus on how the author's choice of point of view affects your response to the story.

Antonio Cruz and Felix Varga were both seventeen years old. They were so together in friendship that they felt themselves to be brothers. They had known each other since childhood, growing up on the lower east side of Manhattan in the same tenement building on Fifth Street between Avenue A and Avenue B.

Antonio was fair, lean, and lanky, while Felix was dark, short, and husky. Antonio's hair was always falling over his eyes, while Felix wore his black hair in a natural Afro style.

Each youngster had a dream of someday becoming lightweight champion of the world. Every chance they had the boys worked out, sometimes at the Boy's Club on 10th Street and Avenue A and sometimes at the pro's gym on 14th Street. Early morning sunrises would find them running along the East River Drive, wrapped in sweat shirts, short towels around their necks, and handkerchiefs Apache style around their foreheads. . . .

Each had fought many bouts representing their community and had won gold-plated medals plus a silver and bronze medallion. The difference was in their style. Antonio's lean form and long reach made him the better boxer, while Felix's short and muscular frame made him the better slugger. Whenever they had met in the ring for sparring sessions, it had always been hot and heavy.

Now, after a series of elimination bouts, they had been informed that they were to meet each other in the division finals that were scheduled for the seventh of August, two weeks away—the winner to represent the Boys Club in the Golden Gloves Championship Tournament.

The two boys continued to run together along the East River Drive. But even when joking with each other, they both sensed a wall rising between them.

One morning less than a week before their bout, they met as usual for their daily work-out. They fooled around with a few jabs at the air, slapped skin, and then took off, running lightly along the dirty East River's edge.

Antonio glanced at Felix who kept his eyes purposely straight ahead, pausing from time to time to do some fancy leg work while throwing one-twos followed by upper cuts to an imaginary jaw. Antonio then beat the air with a barrage of body blows and short devastating lefts with an overhand jaw-breaking right.

After a mile or so, Felix puffed and said, "Let's stop a while, bro. I think we both got something to say to each other."

Antonio nodded. It was not natural to be acting as though nothing unusual was happening when two ace-boon buddies were going to be blasting . . . each other within a few short days.

They rested their elbows on the railing separating them from the river. Antonio wiped his face with his short towel. The sunrise was now creating day.

Felix leaned heavily on the river's railing and stared across to the shores of Brooklyn. Finally, he broke the silence.

"Jesus, man. I don't know how to come out with it."

Antonio helped. "It's about our fight, right?"

"Yeah, right." Felix's eyes squinted at the rising orange sun.

"I've been thinking about it too, *panin*. In fact, since we found out it was going to be me and you, I've been awake at night, pulling punches on you, trying not to hurt you."

"Same here. It ain't natural not to think about the fight. I mean, we both are *cheverote* fighters and we both want to win. But only one of us can win. There ain't no draws in the eliminations."

Felix tapped Antonio gently on the shoulder. "I don't mean to sound like I'm bragging, bro. But I wanna win, fair and square."

Antonio nodded quietly. "Yeah. We both know that in the ring the better man wins. Friend or no friend, brother or no . . ."

Felix finished it for him. "Brother. Tony, let's promise something right here. Okay?"

"If it's fair, *hermano,* I'm for it." Antonio admired the courage of a tug boat pulling a barge five times its welterweight size.

"It's fair, Tony. When we get into the ring, it's gotta be like we never met. We gotta be like two heavy strangers that want the same thing and only one can have it. You understand, don'tcha?"

"*Si,* I know." Tony smiled. "No pulling punches. We go all the way."

"Yeah, that's right. Listen, Tony. Don't you think it's a good idea if we don't see each other until the day of the fight? I'm going to stay with my Aunt Lucy in the Bronx. I can use Gleason's Gym for working out. My manager says he got some sparring partners with more or less your style."

Tony scratched his nose pensively. "Yeah, it would be better for our heads." He held out his hand, palm upward. "Deal?"

"Deal." Felix lightly slapped open skin.

"Ready for some more running?" Tony asked lamely.

"Naw, bro. Let's cut it here. You go on. I kinda like to get things together in my head."

"You ain't worried, are you?" Tony asked.

"No way, man." Felix laughed out loud. "I got too much smarts for that. I just think it's cooler if we split right here. After the fight, we can get it together again like nothing ever happened."

The amigo brothers were not ashamed to hug each other tightly.

"Guess you're right. Watch yourself, Felix. I hear there's some pretty heavy dudes up in the Bronx. *Sauvecito,* okay?"

"Okay. You watch yourself too, *sabe?*"

Tony jogged away. Felix watched his friend disappear from view, throwing rights and lefts. Both fighters had a lot of psyching up to do before the big fight. . . .

Bong! Round three—the final round. Up to now it had been tic-tac-toe, pretty much even. But everyone knew there could be no draw and that this round would decide the winner.

This time, to Felix's surprise, it was Antonio who came out fast, charging across the ring. Felix braced himself but couldn't ward off the barrage of punches. Antonio drove Felix hard against the ropes.

The crowd ate it up. Thus far the two had fought with *mucho corazón.* Felix tapped his gloves and commenced his attack anew. Antonio, throwing boxer's caution to the winds, jumped in to meet him.

Both pounded away. Neither gave an inch and neither fell to the canvas. Felix's left eye was tightly closed. Claret red blood poured from Antonio's nose. They fought toe-to-toe.

The sounds of their blows were loud in contrast to the silence of a crowd gone completely mute. The referee was stunned by their savagery.

Bong! Bong! Bong! The bell sounded over and over again. Felix and Antonio were past hearing. Their blows continued to pound on each other like hailstones.

Finally the referee and the two trainers pried Felix and Antonio apart. Cold water was poured over them to bring them back to their senses.

They looked around and then rushed toward each other. A cry of alarm surged through Tompkins Square Park. Was this a fight to the death instead of a boxing match?

The fear soon gave way to wave upon wave of cheering as the two *amigos* embraced.

No matter what the decision, they knew they would always be champions to each other.

BONG! BONG! BONG! "Ladies and Gentlemen. *Señores and Señoras.* The winner and representative to the Golden Gloves Tournament of Champions is . . ."

The announcer turned to point to the winner and found himself alone. Arm in arm the champions had already left the ring.

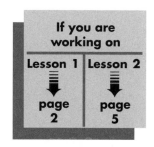

If you are working on

Lesson 1	Lesson 2
⇩	⇩
page 2	page 5

Bette Greene (1934-) grew up in a small town in Arkansas. She studied at Columbia University and in Paris and now lives in Massachusetts. Ms. Greene, the author of many novels for teenagers, is most famous for her first novel, *Summer of My German Soldier*, the story of a Jewish girl who helps an escaped German prisoner of war during World War II. It was named an Outstanding Book of the Year by *The New York Times* and was made into a popular, Emmy-winning television movie. This short story, told from the point of view of a teenage girl's mother, has the strong emotional appeal that is typical of her novels.

An Ordinary Woman

by Bette Greene

I dial the number that for more than twenty years has been committed to memory and then begin counting the rings. One . . . two . . . three . . . four . . . five . . . six —. . . What's wrong with —

"Newton North High School, good morning."

"Jeannette? Oh, good morning. This is Armanda Brooks. Look, I may be a few minutes late today. Something came up — no, dear, I'm fine, thanks for asking. It's just a . . . a family matter that I must take care of. I shouldn't be more than ten to twenty minutes late for my first class, and I was wondering if you'd kindly ask one of my students, Dani Nikas, to start reading to the class from where we left off in *The Chocolate War*? . . . Oh, that would help a lot. . . . Thanks, Jeannette, thanks a lot."

Aimlessly I wander from bookcase to armchair to table and finally to the large French window that looks out upon my street. Like yesterday and so many yesterdays before, my neighbor's paneled station wagon is parked in the exact spot halfway up their blue asphalt driveway. And today, like yesterday, Roderick Street continues to be shaded by a combination of mature oaks and young Japanese maples.

How can everything look the same when nothing really feels the same? Good Lord, Mandy Brooks, how old are you going to have to be before you finally get it into your head that the world takes no interest in your losses?

The grandfather clock in the hall begins chiming out the hour of seven and suddenly fear gnaws at my stomach. What am I afraid of now? For one thing, all those minutes. At least thirty of them that I'll have to face alone, here, with just my thoughts.

Calm down now! It's only thirty minutes. Why, the

last thing the locksmith said last night was that he'd be here first thing this morning. "Between seven thirty and eight for sure!"

Anyway, nobody can make me think when I still have the kitchen counter to wipe and breakfast dishes to put into the dishwasher. Thinking hasn't come this hard since Steve's death on the eve of our eighteenth anniversary. That was major league pain all right, but so dear God is this. So is this . . . .

No time for that now—no time! Tidying up the kitchen is the only thing that I want to think about. But upon entering the kitchen, I see that with the exception of a mug still half full of undrunk coffee, there is really nothing to do. I pour the now cold coffee into the sink before examining the mug with all those miniature red hearts revolving around the single word MOM.

It was a gift from Caren and not all that long ago either. Maybe a year, but certainly no more than a year ago. But even then I had had suspicions that something wasn't right. Maybe without Caren's loving gift coming at me out of the blue, I would have followed my instincts and checked things out. But frankly I doubt that. The thing is that I wanted—needed to believe in my daughter.

And going through her drawers in search of I-knew-not-what offended me. It goes against my sense that everybody, even a seventeen-year-old, deserves privacy. . . .

Outside a truck door slams. I look at my watch. Five minutes after seven. Could he be here already? I rush to the window to see a white panel truck with black lettering—NEWTON CENTRE LOCKSMITHS—at my curb. And a young man, not all that much older than my seniors, is walking briskly up the front walk.

As he takes the front steps, two at a time, I already have the door open. "I really appreciate your being so prompt. You're even earlier than you said you'd be."

"It wasn't me you spoke to. It was my dad, but when he said that a Mrs. Brooks had to have her locks changed first thing in the morning so she wouldn't be late for school, well, I just knew it had to be you."

"Good Lord, I remember you!" I say, grabbing his hand. "You were a student of mine!"

He nods and smiles as he holds tightly to my hand. "You were my favorite English teacher." Then his eyes drop as though he is taking in the intricate pattern of the hall rug. "I guess you were my all-time favorite teacher!"

"Oh, that's lovely of you to say, David—your name is David?"

He grins as though I have given him a present. "David, yes. David Robinson. Hey, you know that's something! You must have had a few hundred students since me. I graduated Newton North two years ago. . . . How do you remember all of your students?"

I hear myself laughing. Laughter, it feels strange, but nice. Very nice. "You give me too much credit, you really do. I'm afraid I can't remember all my students. There have been so many in twenty years. But I think I can probably remember all the students that I really liked."

He takes in the compliment silently as I ask, "Your dad said it wouldn't take long putting in a new cylinder?"

"Ten minutes, Mrs. Brooks. Fifteen at the outside. . . . How many sets of keys will you need?"

"Set of keys?" I feel my composure begin to dissolve. Suddenly I'm not sure I can trust my voice, so like an early grade-school child, I hold out a finger. Only one finger.

As I quickly turn to start up the stairs, the acrid smell of yesterday's fire once again strikes my nostrils. Never mind that now! This isn't the time for thinking about what was . . . and especially not the time for thinking about what could have been.

But even as I command myself to go nonstop into my bedroom for purse and checkbook and then quickly back down the stairs again, I see myself disobeying.

So I stand there at the threshold of Caren's room staring at the two things that had been burned by fire. Her canopy bed rests on only three legs and where the fourth leg once was there is a basketball-size burn in the thick lime-colored rug. Her stereo, records, wall-to-wall posters of rock stars, like everything else in this room, are layered with soot.

I remember now that one of the firemen remarked last night that it was sure a lucky thing that the fire had been contained before it reached the mattress. "You just don't know," he said, "how lucky you are."

How lucky I am? Am I lucky? That's what they used to call me back when I was a high school cheerleader. It all started when Big Joe Famori looked up from the huddle and didn't see me on the sidelines so he bellowed out, "Where's lucky Mandy?"

But if I really was lucky twenty-five years ago for Big Joe and the Malden Eagles, then why can't I be just a little lucky for the ones I've really loved? 'Cause with a little luck, Steve's tumor could just as easily have been benign, but it wasn't. And with a little luck, Caren could have got her highs from life instead of from drugs. But she didn't.

Luck. Dumb, unpredictable luck. Maybe there's no such thing as luck. Or maybe I used up all my precious supply on Big Joe Famori and the Malden Eagles. Is that where I failed you, Caren? Not having any more luck to give you?

When you were a little thing, I knew exactly how to make your tears go away. A fresh diaper, a bottle of warm milk, or maybe a song or two while you slept in my arms. That was all the magic I owned, but in your eyes, all power rested in my hands. For you, my love, I lit the stars at night and every morning called forth the eastern sun.

Probably very early on, I should have warned you that your mother was a very ordinary woman with not a single extraordinary power to her name. But, honey, I don't think you would have believed me because I think you needed me to be a miracle mom every bit as much as I needed to be one.

The trouble, though, didn't start until you grew larger and your needs, too, grew in size. And the all-protecting arms that I once held out to you couldn't even begin to cover these new and larger dimensions. Because it wasn't wet diapers or empty stomachs that needed attending to. It was, instead, pride that was shaken and dreams that somehow got mislaid.

So I see now that what from the very beginning I was dedicated to doing, became, of course, impossible to do. And maybe, just maybe, somewhere in the most submerged recesses of our brains, way down there where light or reason rarely penetrates, neither of us could forgive my impotence.

"Mrs. Brooks," David calls from downstairs. "You're all set now."

"I'll be right down." And then without moving from the spot at the threshold, I speak softly to the empty room. Or, more to the point, to the girl who once lived and laughed and dreamed within these walls. "Caren, dear Caren, I don't know if you're in the next block or the next state. I don't know if I'll see you by nightfall or if I'll see you ever.

"But if you someday return to slip your key into a lock that it no longer fits, I hope you'll understand. Understand, at least, that I'm not barring you, but only what you have become.

"You should know too that if I actually possessed just

a little of that magic that you once believed in, I wouldn't have a moment's trouble deciding how to spend it. I'd hold you to me until your crying stops and your need for drugs fades away."

David Robinson stands at the bottom of the hall stairs, waiting for me. "You know, you're a lucky lady, Mrs. Brooks," he says, dropping a single brass key into my hand. "You're not even going to be late for class."

Although the center hall has always been the darkest room in the house, I fumble through my purse for my sunglasses before answering. "Yes, David," I say, peering at him through smoke-gray glasses. "People have always said that about me."

If you are
working on

Lesson 1	Lesson 2
↓	↓
page 17	page 19

Reviewing *Point of View*

A. Read the story "An Ordinary Woman" on pages 12-16. As you read, write sidenotes that discuss the clues you find and your responses to the point of view. Then use your notes to complete the diagram below.

Identify	Look Back	Respond
Who's telling the story? Which words tell me this?	Can I find thoughts and feelings expressed by the main character? **OR** Can I find story events described by an outside narrator?	How did the author's choice of point of view affect my response to the story?

B. Write the opening paragraph for a story about two family members who work together to overcome a problem. Use the third-person point of view in your paragraph.

Testing *Point of View*

A. The statements below are based on the story "An Ordinary Woman." Fill in the circle next to each true statement. On the lines following each set of statements, explain why you chose the statement you did.

1. ○ The words in the story, *"Aimlessly I wander from bookcase to armchair to table . . ."* tell readers that the narrator is the main character.

   ○ The words in the story, *"Aimlessly I wander from bookcase to armchair to table . . ."* tell readers that there is an outside narrator.

   _____

   _____

2. ○ David and Caren probably have the same relationship with the narrator.

   ○ The narrator has vivid memories of her daughter as a young child.

   _____

   _____

3. ○ The story focuses mostly on the feelings of the narrator, her daughter, and her husband.

   ○ The story focuses mostly on the feelings of the narrator.

   _____

   _____

B. What might you learn if the story had been told from the daughter's point of view?

   _____

   _____

   _____

   _____

   _____

**To begin
Lesson 2
⬇
page
5**

Reviewing **Multiple Meaning Words**

A. Reread the story "An Ordinary Woman" on pages 12-16. As you read, circle words that are multiple meaning words, such as *spot, table,* and *mug* on pages 12-13. Choose one of these words or one of your own to complete the diagram below.

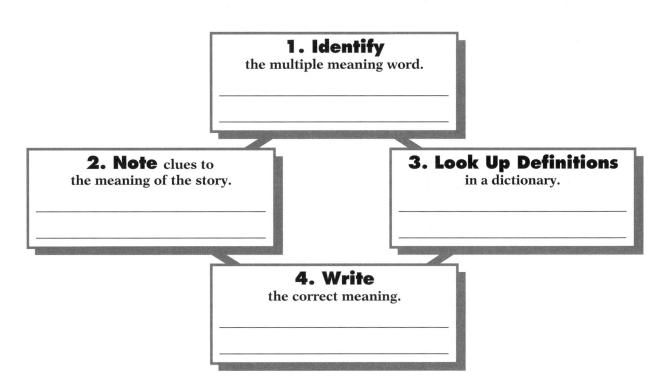

1. Identify
the multiple meaning word.

2. Note clues to
the meaning of the story.

3. Look Up Definitions
in a dictionary.

4. Write
the correct meaning.

B. Find the definitions for the word *ordinary* in the dictionary. Why do you think the author chose to use the word in the title "An Ordinary Woman"? Write your response below. Use details from the story to support your response.

_____

_____

_____

_____

_____

_____

_____

Testing *Multiple Meaning Words*

A. In each sentence below, the word or phrase in bold type has multiple meanings. Read each sentence and think about the way in which the word or phrase is used. Put a check in the box next to the correct meaning for the word as it is used in the sentence. Then on the lines provided, list clues from the sentence that helped you make your choice.

1. Because of an accident at Fourth Street and Washington Boulevard, the traffic in the city was **tied up** for hours.

   [ ] secured with string or rope
   [ ] kept from moving
   [ ] completed, finished

   _____

2. The **store** was out of bread this morning.

   [ ] a place where groceries are purchased
   [ ] a stockpile of articles gathered for future use
   [ ] to put things away in a closet or trunk

   _____

3. A driving **range** in the middle of a city park is a great idea.

   [ ] a series of things in a line
   [ ] the limits within which something can move or vary
   [ ] an open region in which animals roam
   [ ] a place where golf is practiced

   _____

B. Choose one of the multiple meaning words above. Use the word in a paragraph. In your writing, use a meaning of the word that is different from the meaning that you checked above.

   _____

   _____

   _____

   _____

   _____

   _____

   _____

   _____

Unit TWO

BECOMING AN ACTIVE READER

Good readers of **science fiction stories** are alert and thoughtful readers. They think about what they already know and compare it to what they find out as they read.

Using Skills and Strategies

Inferring an author's unstated message, or **theme**, will help you read science fiction thoughtfully. To make inferences about the theme you might ask: What do I know or what have I experienced that will help me understand what is happening in the story? What do these events tell me about the author's overall message?

Identifying the **sequence** of events in a story helps you better understand what is happening to the story characters and why. To follow the sequence, you might ask: What important event starts the story? Which events in the middle are important? What is the final outcome?

In this unit, the skills of **making inferences** about an author's **theme** and identifying **sequence** will help you become an active and thoughtful reader.

Reading Science Fiction Stories

As you read science fiction stories, think about concepts in science you already know. Read actively, trying to relate those ideas to the imaginative details in the stories. Enjoy the stories as you read. Find a place where you can read comfortably. Take a few deep breaths and relax. Then enter the strange world of science turned into incredible, thought-provoking stories.

Responding to Science Fiction

Good readers respond to details in science fiction stories. Write your responses as you read the two stories in this unit, "Lemmings" and "Tank." Writing sidenotes will help you remember the stories as you discuss them with classmates.

Making Inferences

| *Lesson 3* | Introducing page 22 | Practicing page 23 | Applying page 24 | Reviewing page 35 | Testing page 36 |

Introducing Strategies

To understand short stories, readers often have to read between the lines and think about what the author does not say. This process of figuring out the missing information is called **making inferences.** Good readers use evidence from the story and their own background knowledge to make inferences.

The puzzle pieces below show how readers make inferences to figure out the author's underlying message, or theme, in a story. To do this, readers think about the clues in the story such as the characters' words and actions and the events in the plot. Then they relate these clues to their own experiences.

Character's Words and Actions, and Story Events **+** The Reader's Thoughts and Experiences **=** Inferences About the Theme of the Story

Reading the Story

Read the story "Lemmings" on pages 28-29 and the sidenotes on page 28. These notes show how one good reader used clues about characters and events to make inferences about the theme. After reading, complete the items below.

1. Which clues is the reader using to make a connection between what is happening in the story and what the author may be saying?

_____

_____

2. What prior knowledge did the reader use when making inferences about the story?

_____

_____

Practicing *Making Inferences*

A. Circle the letter in front of the phrase that best completes each statement about the story. Then on the lines that follow, support your answer by identifying clues from the story or relating it to something you already know.

1. The people on the beach enter the water, even if they cannot swim, because
   a. they want to escape the summer heat.
   b. there is nothing left for them on land.
   c. the police have sponsored a swimming contest.
   d. everyone else is doing it.

   _____

   _____

2. Both Reordon and Carmack enter the water because
   a. they, like all humans, have no reason to live.
   b. the idea of acting like lemmings is entertaining to them.
   c. each believes he can swim better than the other and survive longer.
   d. they, like lemmings, seem to do it without thinking.

   _____

   _____

3. Carmack suggests that people act like lemmings when they
   a. leave the Scandinavian countries.
   b. do not learn how to swim fast or far.
   c. have eaten too much of their food supply.
   d. can't control resources needed to survive.

   _____

   _____

B. Write a paragraph describing a time when you or someone you know experienced peer pressure. Describe how you overcame the problem.

   _____

   _____

   _____

   _____

   _____

Applying *Making Inferences*

A. Read the passage below. Then answer the questions that follow.

> *Loud arguments began each morning at the market square in the village where Moira and Jake lived. As morning turned into afternoon, more and more people gathered and took sides in these arguments. The sound grew deafening.*
> *"They are no better than wild animals," Jake said.*
> *"Well, there is plenty to argue about," Moira replied. "The mayor won't enforce the laws. The street sweeper refuses to sweep the square. The village is going to ruin."*
> *"People can live better than that," Jake remarked, looking for agreement from Moira.*
> *"No, they can't," Moira surprisingly announced.*
> *Jake and Moira's words grew louder as they tried to answer each other. Their voices echoed throughout the village.*

1. What can you infer about the author's central message, or theme, through the actions of the people and the words of Moira and Jake?

_____

_____

2. Explain the clues that helped you make your inference. Include words or phrases from the passage along with what you already know.

_____

_____

B. Write a brief story that has a theme or makes a statement about ways people act. Provide clues to this theme through the characters' words and actions and the events in the plot.

_____

_____

_____

_____

_____

_____

To review
↓
page
35

Sequence

| *Lesson 4* | **Introducing** page 25 | **Practicing** page 26 | **Applying** page 27 | **Reviewing** page 37 | **Testing** page 38 |

Introducing Strategies

Authors create a certain effect in their stories by arranging the events in a certain order, or **sequence.** Sometimes one event may lead to another event that leads to a specific final event or outcome. Presenting events in chronological order, or the order in which they occur, is one way authors may choose to tell a story. The diagram below shows how readers can follow the order of events in a story.

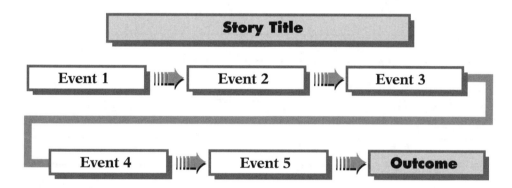

Story Title

Event 1 → Event 2 → Event 3

Event 4 → Event 5 → **Outcome**

Reading the Story

Reread the story "Lemmings" on pages 28-29. As you read, underline and number the important events in chronological order. Then answer the questions below.

1. List three events that occurred in the story in their correct order.

_____

_____

_____

2. What is the final event or outcome of the story?

_____

_____

_____

_____

_____

Practicing **Sequence**

A. The statements below are about the story "Lemmings," but they are not totally correct. Rewrite each statement so that it reflects the correct order of events in the story.

1. As the story opens, Carmack compares human behavior to the behavior of lemmings.

_____

_____

_____

2. At the end of the story, a woman in a fur coat goes into the water and drowns.

_____

_____

3. Reordon and Carmack rush into the water as soon as they see people drowning.

_____

_____

4. At the end of the story, only Carmack remains on the beach.

_____

_____

B. Do you think the story would have been as effective if the sequence of events was changed and you knew right away what would happen? Explain why or why not.

_____

_____

_____

_____

_____

_____

_____

Applying **Sequence**

A. Read the passage below. Then answer the questions that follow.

> Like every other Sunday in the warm season, Renatta Astrack and her young ones walked outside the Ringed City. But this was not a typical walk. On this walk, they entered the Forbidden Mountains in search of the missing Nabin Astrack.
>
> At first, Renatta could not hear any sounds at all. But she knew that a strange people called "homo sapiens" lived in the mountains. They were known for their strange sounds, which put people into trances, called "music."
>
> After several hours, as Renatta climbed over a rock ledge, she heard a dreamy sound come from above. She and her young ones could not help but follow the enchanting sound.

1. What did Renatta hear when she first entered the Forbidden Mountains?

_____

_____

2. When did Renatta hear "music"?

_____

_____

B. Write a paragraph about an imaginary incident. In your paragraph, describe the events in the order in which they occur so that they lead up to the final outcome.

_____

_____

_____

_____

_____

_____

_____

_____

_____

_____

To review

page 37

Richard Matheson (1926-) was born in Allendale, New Jersey. His numerous works have been mostly fantasy and horror stories. Matheson also has written several successful screenplays, including *The Incredible Shrinking Man* and *The Duel.* Matheson uses an unusual event—the mass suicide of thousands of small arctic rodents, called lemmings—as the basis for this science fiction story.

Lemmings

by Richard Matheson

The notes in the margin show how one reader made inferences about the story theme by noting the characters' words and story events and by relating them to what he or she already knew.

"Where do they all come from?" Reordon asked.

"Everywhere," said Carmack.

They were standing on the coast highway. As far as they could see there was nothing but cars. Thousands of cars were jammed bumper to bumper and pressed side to side. The highway was solid with them.

"There come some more," said Carmack.

The two policemen looked at the crowd of people walking toward the beach. Many of them talked and laughed. Some of them were very quiet and serious. But they all walked toward the beach.

Reordon shook his head. "I don't get it," he said for the hundredth time that week. "I just don't get it."

Carmack shrugged.

"Don't think about it," he said. "It's happening. What

▶ else is there?"

Carmack says "Don't think about it," when his partner questions what's happening. Maybe these people are not thinking—just like the lemmings seem to act without thinking.

"But it's crazy."

"Well, there they go," said Carmack.

As the two policemen watched, the crowd of people moved across the gray sands of the beach and walked into the water. Some of them started swimming. Most of them couldn't because of their clothes. Carmack saw a young woman flailing at the water and dragged down by the fur coat she was wearing.

In several minutes they were all gone. The two policemen stared at the place where the people had walked into the water.

"How long does it go on?" Reordon asked.

"Until they're gone, I guess," said Carmack.

"But why?"

"Lemmings" must have something to do with the point the author is trying to make. I know that lemmings move in large groups and fall to their deaths over cliffs and in rivers when there are too many of them.

▶ "You ever read about the lemmings?" Carmack asked.

"No."

"They're rodents who live in the Scandinavian countries. They keep breeding until all their food supply is gone. Then they move across the country, ravaging everything in their way. When they reach the sea they keep going. They swim until their strength is gone. Millions of them."

"You think that's what this is?" asked Reordon.

"Maybe," said Carmack.

"People aren't rodents!" Reordon said angrily.

Carmack didn't answer.

They stood on the edge of the highway waiting but nobody appeared.

"Where are they?" asked Reordon.

"Maybe they've all gone in," Carmack said.

"All of them?"

"It's been going on for more than a week," Carmack said. "People could have gotten here from all over. Then there are the lakes."

Reordon shuddered. "All of them," he said.

"I don't know," said Carmack, "but they've been coming right along until now."

"Oh, God," said Reordon.

Carmack took out a cigarette and lit it. "Well," he said, "what now?"

Reordon sighed. "Us?" he said.

"You go," Carmack said. "I'll wait a while and see if there's anyone else."

"All right." Reordon put his hand out. "Good-by, Carmack," he said.

They shook hands. "Good-by, Reordon," Carmack said.

He stood smoking his cigarette and watching his friend walk across the gray sand of the beach and into the water until it was over his head. He saw Reordon swim a few dozen yards before he disappeared.

After a while he put out his cigarette and looked around. Then he walked into the water too.

A million cars stood empty along the beach.

As you read the rest of the story, think about the characters and events. Then write your own inferences about the theme.

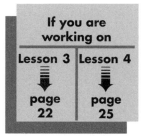

If you are working on

Lesson 3	Lesson 4
⬇	⬇
page 22	page 25

Lemmings ■ **29**

Francis Izzo works for an advertising agency. He writes copy for ads produced by the agency. In his spare time, he writes science fiction stories like this one. His work has been published in major magazines as well as in collections of science fiction.

Tank

As you read, make notes about the story details that help you infer the author's message or theme. Write your notes in the margins. Remember to relate the details to your own experiences.

by Francis E. Izzo

Davis slammed the flipper and watched the steel ball go skittering up toward the 500 target.

"Go, baby!"

Five hundred more points and it would be free-game time.

The ball kissed the target, but lacked the strength to register on the scoreboard. . . .

This time he tensed his body, ran through some unconscious calculations, and pushed the flipper hard, while lifting the underbelly of the machine with a practiced jerk.

"Tilt," sneered the box.

He looked away in disgust. In the arcade, he could hear the music of the pinball jockeys: bells and buzzers, whirs and clicks, thuds and springing noises.

He knew every machine in the place and had won on most. . . .

It all led him to one conclusion: a computer hooked to a TV screen couldn't do what those simple steel pinballs could. It couldn't provide him with an infinite variety of challenge. The electronics always had a pattern.

He simply couldn't understand what drew the people to the electronic screens. But they were there day after day in increasing numbers, plugged into the blip-blip-bleep of the cathode tubes. . . .

But for him, it was time to go back to Lady Luck. That pinball had been giving him a lot of trouble lately. It had a particularly treacherous combination of holes, targets, and bumpers that kept his senses spinning with every roll.

On his way back up the electronic alley, Davis noticed something new.

There was a booth with a seat and a screen. On the front it lacked the psychedelic paint of most of the games. No lights flashing. Simply painted dull green, with the word TANK printed in block letters on the entrance.

Fresh meat. A new game to master, then throw away to the uncultured palates of the amateurs.

He climbed into the booth, slightly nervous in anticipation of breaking in a brand-new machine.

He looked for the directions. They weren't in sight. Neither was the coin slot. They were probably still setting this one up.

It looked a little different from the other electronic sets. With a small slit screen, similar to the kind on a real tank, it had a panel of control wheels and levers marked with elevation marks, and many other controls he had never seen on a game before.

Davis ran his fingers over the seat. Leather, and quite worn for a new machine. There was a pungent odor in the booth, a kind of locker-room smell.

The controls looked sophisticated. He imagined that this game might turn out to be some fun, once they set it up.

Just as he was leaving to return to the pinballs, he noticed one of the control levers had some writing on it.

It said, "ON."

When he pulled it, the door to the booth closed. A light was activated above his head. A sign flashed, "FASTEN SEAT BELT."

Not bad.

Davis reached across the seat and pulled up a heavy leather strap across his waist. It tightened and firmly planted him in his seat.

Another light went on.

"PLACE HEADGEAR."

Directly above his head there was a leather headpiece dangling from a wire.

Nice effects, he thought, putting on the headgear. The light flicked off, then another one came on. It was bright, piercing blue button that glowed with the word "START."

When he pushed it, three things happened: an engine started rumbling and shaking his seat, the screen lit up in full color *(color!),* and his booth started to move. Or at least it seemed to move.

Quickly he felt for gas and brake and found them in a comfortable spot on the floor. His hands went instinctively for the steering wheel. It was a bit like one of the old tanks he'd studied in basic training.

The rumbling in the booth increased as he pushed the gas pedal. Soon it was almost deafening.

On the screen, there was an open field, bouncing up and down to the movements of his booth.

OK, he thought, *if they call this game TANK, I should be seeing some tanks one of these days.*

Davis grabbed for the seat belt, but it was jammed. The heat was becoming unbearable.

Suddenly he heard an odd scraping noise coming from over his head.

He looked up, his eyes tearing profusely from the smoke. The sound of metal giving way rang through his ears, and sunlight burned through a momentary hole over his head.

Something fell in, then the crack of sunlight was shut off.

He recognized it and was instantly sick.

Grenade.

He was clawing frantically at the seat straps when it went off with a dull thud.

There was no explosion. No impact. No flash. Just a single piece of cardboard issued from the metal casing of the grenade.

And it said, neatly printed in block letters:

"GAME OVER."

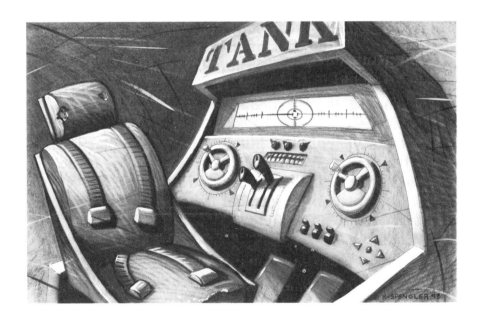

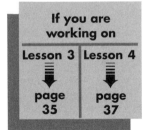

If you are
working on

Lesson 3	Lesson 4
↓	↓
page 35	page 37

Reviewing *Making Inferences*

A. Read the story "Tank" on pages 30-34. As you read, make some notes in the margins about the author's message, or theme. Underline any of Davis's thoughts or actions that might be clues. Add your own experiences. Then use your notes to complete the chart below.

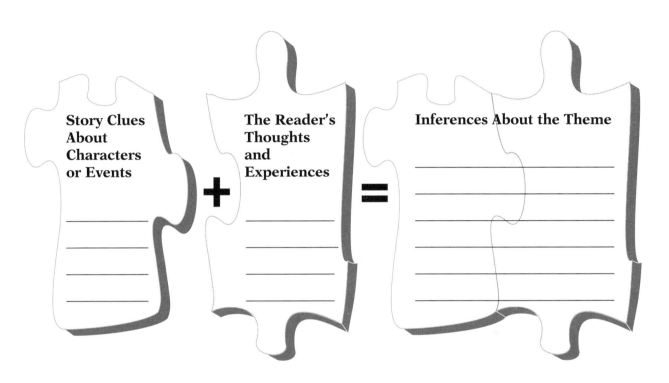

Story Clues About Characters or Events

+

The Reader's Thoughts and Experiences

=

Inferences About the Theme

B. What point do you think the author is trying to make in this story? Use clues from the story and what you know to support your ideas.

_____

_____

_____

_____

_____

_____

_____

_____

_____

Testing Making Inferences

A. Each inference below is based on the story "Tank" on pages 30-34. Fill in the oval next to each statement about the theme that makes sense. Then, on the lines provided, explain why you did or did not select each item.

⭕ 1. Electronic games are dangerous because they can make what's not real seem real.

_____

_____

⭕ 2. Electronic games are programmed, patterned, predictable—and fun.

_____

_____

⭕ 3. Computer technology has unlimited potential to expand the human mind.

_____

_____

⭕ 4. Pinball machines are more challenging than computer games.

_____

_____

B. Think about how technology has affected your life. Write a brief paragraph involving a video game or some electronic device. In your paragraph, give the reader clues to the underlying theme, or the major point, you are making about technology.

_____

_____

_____

_____

_____

_____

_____

_____

To begin Lesson 4 ⬇ page 25

Reviewing *Sequence*

A. Reread the story "Tank" on pages 30-34. As you read, think about the major events as they build up to the final outcome. Begin on page 30 at the point where Davis notices the game labeled TANK. Follow the events by completing the diagram below. If necessary, add additional boxes to complete the chain.

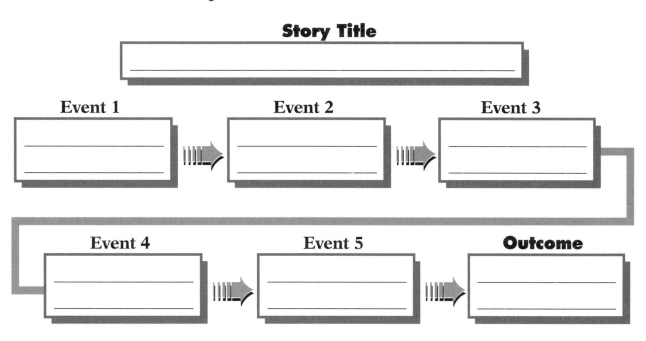

Story Title

Event 1 → Event 2 → Event 3

Event 4 → Event 5 → **Outcome**

B. Describe an exciting electronic video game that you have played. Tell about the outcome of the game and explain the events that led to that outcome.

_____

_____

_____

_____

_____

_____

_____

_____

_____

_____

_____

Testing Sequence

A. The incomplete paragraph below is a summary of events from the story "Tank." Read the passage through. Then go back and fill in each blank with the word from the list that best completes the summary.

thunderous

but

over

starts

grenade

second

when

finds

challenging

Suddenly Davis sees a new game in the arcade, a booth labeled "Tank." He _____ the new game tempting— it looks so much more realistic than the other electronic games. He straps himself into the leather seat and _____ the game up. A small German Tiger comes after him immediately. Under fire, Davis manages to get the tank gun's range and distance right: he destroys the Tiger. The _____ tank is a heavier, more dangerous model. Davis finds the combat much more _____ when the _____ blast of an enemy shell slams him into the controls, cutting a bleeding gash over his eye.

Davis runs from his opponent _____ an enemy shell destroys one of his treads. Davis turns to fight, and the tanks exchange point-blank fire. _____ Davis returns to consciousness after the blast, a _____ is dropped into his tank. For Davis, the game is _____.

B. Write a brief summary statement reflecting the sequence in a portion of the story "Tank." Then delete three words from the summary and leave blanks for a partner to fill in.

_____

_____

_____

_____

Unit THREE

BECOMING AN ACTIVE READER

Good readers are informed readers. **Editorials** help readers stay informed on current issues. Good readers use editorials to find out both sides of an issue.

Using Skills and Strategies

Looking for main ideas while **reading editorials** will help you identify the writer's position. You might ask: What is the topic? What is the writer's position? What major ideas support the writer's position?

Scanning for **key words** will help you identify the topic of an editorial. Readers use key words to figure out what the editorial's position is on the topic.

In this unit, the skills of **reading editorials** and identifying **key words** will help you read more actively.

The Editorial: The Writer's Voice

Editorials usually reflect the political viewpoints of the newspapers in which they appear. Editorials provide people from diverse cultures a way to compare their opinions and beliefs to those of others. Editorials can present an issue from a new or different point of view. By reading editorials, you can learn a great deal about the issues of concern to people from cultures and backgrounds that are similar to and different from your own.

Responding to Editorials

Good readers usually find themselves responding to the editorial's position on the topic. As readers respond, they compare their own position to the writer's. Readers may agree or disagree, based on their own experiences and feelings. It is important to jot down your responses as you read the two editorials in this unit, "What Can Be Learned from Latino Political Gains" and "Preserving Native American Culture Should Be a National Concern." Discuss your responses with your classmates.

Reading Editorials

Introducing Strategies

Editorials take a position on a topic and try to persuade readers to agree with that position. The editorial writer makes some major points to support the position being presented. The purpose of most editorials is to convince readers in a specific audience to take some action based on the information provided.

The diagram below shows how readers organize their thinking when **reading editorials.** First they identify the topic and the writer's position in the topic. Then they identify major points that support the writer's position.

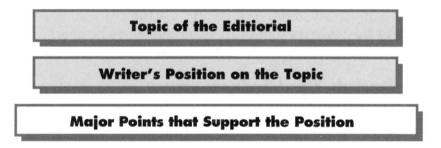

Topic of the Editorial

Writer's Position on the Topic

Major Points that Support the Position

Reading the Editorial

Read the editorial entitled "What Can be Learned from Latino Political Gains" on pages 46-48 and the sidenotes on pages 46-47. These notes show how one good reader identified Mr. Sanchez's position on the topic and some details that support his position. After reading, complete the items below.

1. What has the reader identified as the topic and the writer's position on the topic?

_____

_____

2. List two main details the reader identified that support the writer's position.

_____

_____

Practicing *Reading Editorials*

A. The incomplete sentences below are based on the editorial "What Can Be Learned from Latino Political Gains." Circle the letter of the choice that best completes each sentence. Then on the lines that follow, tell more about the author's feelings about this information.

1. The topic of this editorial is
   a. Peru.   c. political power.
   b. registered voters.   d. Henry Cisneros.

   _____

   _____

2. According to the author, the most important step Latinos can take to gain political representation is to
   a. immigrate.   c. be patient.
   b. vote.   d. write.

   _____

   _____

3. In the long run, some of the most important political gains for Latinos start with results from
   a. local elections.   c. national elections.
   b. voters' polls.   d. political appointments.

   _____

   _____

B. Do you agree or disagree with the author's position in this editorial? Use details from the article that helped persuade you to agree or disagree.

   _____

   _____

   _____

   _____

   _____

   _____

   _____

   _____

Applying *Reading Editorials*

A. Read the following editorial from a school newspaper. Then answer the questions that follow.

This year, like all other years, the school board in our community will be making important decisions. In the past, teachers and parents have come to board meetings to express their views on important matters. But what about the students? Should they take time to share their feelings and ideas with board members?

Martha Sanchez, a ninth-grade student, wrote a letter to the board. She also attended a recent meeting. Martha helped persuade the board to approve a new theater program for South Middle School. Albert Patell, a tenth-grade student, wrote to a board member. He explained how important the soccer team is to his younger brother and other students at North Middle School. The board, moved by his letter, set aside funds for new soccer team uniforms. They're on order right now.

Letters and other signs of interest from students can influence how the board votes. And the board's decisions will affect the success of our schools.

1. What is the writer's position on the topic of this editorial?

_____

_____

2. What information supports the writer's opinion?

_____

_____

_____

B. Write a brief letter to your school board members to persuade them to act on an issue you feel is important to the school. Begin your letter here.

To review
↓
page
51

_____

_____

_____

_____

_____

_____

Key Words

Lesson 6	Introducing page 43	Practicing page 44	Applying page 45	Reviewing page 53	Testing page 54

Introducing Strategies

Before reading editorials, a good reader may scan the article to find some **key words.** Key words are important. They give the reader an idea about the topic of the editorial. Key words can set the stage by signaling the tone of the article, the audience, and the purpose for writing. To find key words, readers scan the title, the introduction, and the first sentence of each paragraph.

The chart below shows how one reader identified and responded to key words in the editorial on page 46.

Where to Look	**Key Words**	**What Key Words Tell the Reader**
Introduction	*vote*	The editorial might be about U.S. citizenship.
Title	*Latino*	The author wants Latinos to have power.
First Sentence	*politicians*	This editorial is about politics.
Other	*Latino vote*	Italic print stresses author's message

Reading the Editorial

Reread the editorial "What Can Be Learned from Latino Political Gains" on pages 46-48. As you read, underline any key words you identify. Then answer the questions below.

1. List four key words you identified in the editorial.

_____

_____

2. What do these words tell you about the topic of the editorial?

_____

_____

Practicing Key Words

A. Read each incomplete sentence below. Circle the letter in front of the word or words that best completes each sentence. Then on the lines that follow, explain your answer.

1. Key words in the title tell the reader that the topic of the editorial might be
   a. music.   c. government.
   b. education.   d. science.

   _____

   _____

2. The most important key word in the introduction is
   a. U.S. citizen.   c. vote.
   b. Latinos.   d. naturalization.

   _____

   _____

3. What is the most important key word in the first sentence in the sixth paragraph?
   a. lesson   c. importance
   b. another   d. local elections

   _____

   _____

B. Write a paragraph explaining your position on the topic of voting. Underline the key word or words in your paragraph.

   _____

   _____

   _____

   _____

   _____

   _____

   _____

   _____

   _____

Applying **Key Words**

A. As you read the following excerpt from an editorial, underline some of the key words. Then answer the questions below.

When you, the registered voter, ask yourself, "Who is the best candidate for mayor of this city?" the only reasonable answer is Ms. Gladys Cheng. As councilor, Ms. Cheng has brought opportunities and resources to our city. Just one example is Ms. Cheng's innovative jobs' program for teenagers. Many grateful citizens will recall that after every snowstorm last winter, hundreds of teenagers hit the streets, armed with snow shovels. Those teens in Ms. Cheng's program kept the sidewalks safe for pedestrians—especially for children walking to school and for the elderly. Ms. Cheng is clearly a candidate who can get things done. As mayor, Ms. Cheng could do even more for our city.

1. List five key words that you underlined in the article.

_____

_____

2. What do these key words tell you about the editorial?

_____

_____

B. Plan an outline for an editorial. In your plan, write 1) the topic, 2) your position on the topic, 3) some supporting ideas, and 4) the audience. Circle the key words you have written in your outline.

_____

_____

_____

_____

_____

_____

_____

_____

To review

page 53

Leonel Sanchez was born in Peru but moved with his family to the United States as a child. Since 1989 he has worked for southern California newspapers, reporting on topics of particular interest to Latinos. Sanchez is currently going through the process of naturalization, becoming a U.S. citizen—mostly because, as he says, "I want to vote."

The writer says that he wants to become a U.S. citizen in order to vote. Perhaps voting is the topic of the editorial. But what position is he taking on voting? ▶

What Can Be Learned from Latino Political Gains

by Leonel Sanchez

The notes in the margins on pages 46 and 47 show how one reader identified the topic of the editorial, the writer's position on the topic, and some of the major points supporting his position.

Powerful politicians have a new responsibility today. When they appoint people to important positions, they must make sure that the entire population is appropriately represented. As the cultural backgrounds of the people in the United States become more diverse, so, too, must the cultural backgrounds of our appointed officials. Native Americans, Latinos, Asian Americans, African Americans . . . all of these groups should have representatives in positions of power.

Here he feels that it's very important for Latinos to vote in order to gain political power. I think his position is that cultural groups need political representation and power.

Voters have the same responsibility as powerful politicians do. We, too, must make sure that we have representation. This means that we must vote for and elect those who truly represent us—our ethnicity, our values, and our needs.

In the 1990s, the Latino community is beginning to feel more comfortable about the political power it has gained. How can we increase that power? What can other groups learn from our successes?

The most important lesson is the importance of voting. Voting is the basis for political success. For example, Latino victories in the area of appointments occurred when President Clinton chose Federico Peña to be Secretary of Transportation and Henry Cisneros to be Secretary of Housing and Urban Development.

Latinos appointed to important jobs by President Clinton first won local elections with the help of Latino voters. This supports the writer's position that voting is the key to political success.

Yet, President Clinton shouldn't receive the credit for putting these leaders into positions of power. The credit should go to Latino voters. Both men had won important local and state elections—*with the help of the Latino vote* before they received national attention. Cisneros was elected mayor of San Antonio four times during the 1980s. His first victory came because the city's heavily

Latino population turned out to vote for him. In contrast, Peña did not have a large Latino voting population that he could tap when he ran for mayor of Denver in 1983. However, Latino leaders were active in pushing Latino voters to turn out at the polls. Peña won the race by just 6,000 votes. It is no coincidence that this is the same number of Latinos who signed up to vote during the final days of voter registration. The point is that voters *can* make a difference.

Another lesson to be learned is the importance of local elections, for both voters and politicians. Voters must not dismiss these elections as less important than state or national elections. Each and every election is important. Having representation at the local level is just as important as having representation elsewhere. As of 1993, nearly 4,000 Latinos held elective offices across the country. Some of these elected officials had a great deal of power, even on a local level. One example is Los Angeles County Supervisor Gloria Molina. The county board to which she was elected governs an area with a huge budget—a budget larger than most state budgets. In 1991, Molina, a Mexican American, became the first Latina *ever* to sit on the county board. She was elected because Latino voters paid attention to local politics and turned out to vote.

◀ Gloria Molina won a local election, but she has a powerful job. I can see that is a good example of how important local elections can be.

Running for local positions is important for up-and-coming politicians, too. For example, in 1988, Florida Republican Ileana Ros-Lehtinen became the first Cuban American elected to Congress. She is from Miami, where she held local elected offices before moving into national politics. Miami is a very large district. The support of its heavily Cuban American population is what gave her the victory in 1988.

◀ I'll look for additional points that support this opinion in this editorial.

A final lesson that all groups, including Latinos, must learn is *never to be satisfied*. Here are the tasks we must constantly set for ourselves:

As you read the rest of the editorial, write your own sidenotes. Focus on major points that support the writer's position on the topic.

1. *We must vote and teach others to vote.* We must spread the message that "voting equals power." In the Latino community, for example, organizations such as the Southwest Voting Registration and Education Project exist simply to give Latinos this important message. They especially aim their efforts at young Latinos. This is important, since the Latino population is younger than the overall U.S. population.

2. *We must gain citizenship.* Since only U.S. citizens can vote, citizenship is the first step to political power.

Yet, huge numbers of immigrants from all over the world are not citizens.

3. *Groups must unify, or work together.* Differences must not be allowed to become harmful. For example, the Latino community is made up of three main groups: Puerto Ricans, Mexican Americans, and Cuban Americans. Bringing these three groups together will not be easy. Cuban Americans tend to be conservative members of the Republican Party. In contrast, Puerto Ricans and Mexican Americans are often more liberal and tend to join the Democratic Party. Despite these differences, the three groups have much in common. They face many similar social, economic, and educational problems that could serve to bring them together. If they can come together as a unified group, Latinos can become an important force in electing leaders. The same point holds true for Asian Americans, who also come from many cultures, and Native Americans, who represent many nations.

4. *We must educate young people and use them as resources.* The contributions of past and present leaders of all backgrounds, both appointed and elected, should be presented in public schools. Young people who haven't reached the voting age should be asked to help register those within their community who are old enough to go to the voting booths. English television stations should work with stations producing shows in languages other than English to present short biographical features about past and present political leaders of various backgrounds. Politics should be presented to young people as an exciting and rewarding career option.

Voters must not sit around waiting for the next high-level appointment. They have to find, train, and elect their own leaders so that they will be ready when and if the call comes from the White House.

If you are working on

Lesson 5	Lesson 6
⬇	⬇
page 40	page 43

Rick Hill, a Tuscarora, is the special assistant to the director of the Smithsonian Institution's National Museum of the American Indian (NMAI). In this editorial, Hill stresses that *all* Americans, not just Native Americans, should help to preserve Native American culture.

Preserving Native American Culture Should Be a National Concern

by Rick Hill

As you read, write some notes about the topic, the writer's position on the topic, and important supporting ideas.

From November 15, 1992, through January 24, 1993, I was the curator of a special exhibit for the National Museum of the American Indian titled "Pathways of Tradition: Indian Insights into Indian Worlds." The artworks included in the exhibit were found within the museum's large collection. They were selected by 28 Native Americans from North, Central, and South America. The result was a 100-piece exhibit of major importance to both Native and non-Native Americans. Why was this exhibit so important?

First, the exhibit allowed viewers to have an insider's look at how Native Americans think about the world. Why is this important? Well, if we Native Americans expect others to support our causes, we must educate people about our cultures. This was the aim of the "Pathways of Tradition" exhibit—to help people understand Native Americans, to hear our voices, feel our emotions, become acquainted with our traditions. Each artwork in the exhibit was labeled by the Native American who selected it. The label explained why the artwork was representative of the selector's specific culture. We stressed to visitors the importance of reading those labels. By looking at each artwork *and* reading about its cultural and historical context, a visitor could gain a great deal of knowledge about Native Americans. That knowledge can bring greater understanding among people.

Second, the exhibit was meant to help keep Native American knowledge, beliefs, and feelings alive for future generations. This is the philosophy of the National Museum of the American Indian. It is a philosophy that we hope more people in the United States will come to share. When Native American culture is kept alive, the whole country is enriched.

That brings me to the third important function of "Pathways of Tradition." This exhibit strove to eliminate stereotypes about Native Americans. It presented our beliefs regarding the earth, the family, and the purpose of art, among others.

The Native American way of thinking about the earth is especially important to understand. We believe that the well-being of humankind is tied to the well-being of the rest of the earth and even of the universe. The artworks that were featured in "Pathways of Tradition" show this way of thinking. In these artworks, the earth is alive. Animals are shown as wise and powerful guides for humans. Circles often appear, representing Native Americans living in harmony with the universe.

To understand us is to understand the importance of family. It is the family that keeps our culture alive. This is one reason that everyday objects were plentiful in the exhibit. For Native Americans, the family is a classroom in which children learn about their culture. Each fork, bowl, and article of clothing can give a message about our beliefs. Therefore, we put much care into the creation of everyday objects.

Finally, to understand us, non-Native Americans must know that we do not isolate art, religion, or culture as activities to be done only at certain times or in certain places. "We have no word for art, we have no word for religion," explained Navajo selector Conrad House, "because there is no need to separate those concepts away from our real life. . . . Real life is all that." Since art is part of the daily lives of Native Americans, "Pathways of Tradition" included objects such as shirts, ceramics, shields, and utensils. The symbols used on these objects often ask for spiritual protection. "The things that we wore, the things that we made—they were made with a prayer," stated Ponca/Osage selector Abe Conklin.

By presenting these and other core Native American beliefs, "Pathways of Tradition" represented a step in the right direction. But the path must continue. Every generation of Native Americans must carry forth the culture in one way or another. Non-Native Americans can help—by learning about our culture and by supporting organizations like the NMAI. Those organizations can continue to educate both non-Native Americans and our own people about our cultures. Through education, we allow the knowledge and values of our ancestors to be carried into the future.

If you are
working on

Lesson 5 | Lesson 6

page
51

page
53

Reviewing **Reading Editorials**

A. Read the editorial entitled "Preserving Native American Culture Should Be a National Concern" on pages 49-50. As you read, make notes in the margins about the topic, the writer's position on the topic, and the supporting ideas. Use the pyramid below to organize your notes.

Topic _____

Writer's Position _____

_____

1. Major Point _____

2. Major Point _____

3. Major Point _____

B. In the editorial, Rick Hill says, "When Native American culture is kept alive, the whole country is enriched." Explain in your own words what this sentence means and whether you agree or disagree.

_____

_____

_____

_____

_____

_____

_____

_____

_____

_____

Testing *Reading Editorials*

A. Fill in the circle next to each true statement about the editorial "Preserving Native American Culture Should Be a National Concern" on pages 49-50. Then, on the lines provided, explain why you selected each statement.

○ The topic of this editorial is preserving Native American culture.

_____

_____

○ The writer's position on the topic is that Native Americans are solely responsible for preserving their own culture.

_____

_____

○ "Pathways of Tradition" is an exhibit that shows how daily life is separate from art in Native American cultures.

_____

_____

○ The writer feels that a good way to understand Native American culture is by learning about Native American art.

_____

_____

B. Imagine you are selecting art for an exhibit about life in your community. What types of objects and paintings might you select for the exhibit? Write a sentence or two, describing each of your choices and why you made each choice.

_____

_____

_____

_____

_____

_____

_____

To begin Lesson 6 ⬇ page 43

Reviewing Key Words

A. Read "Preserving Native American Culture Should Be a National Concern" on pages 49-50. As you read, underline key words that are specific to the subject of the editorial. Then complete the chart below.

Where to Look	Key Words	What Key Words Tell Me
Introduction		
Title		
First Sentence		
Other		

B. Write a brief paragraph describing an especially memorable museum exhibit or community event. In your paragraph, try to convince people of the importance of this event. When you have finished your paragraph, circle the key words.

_____

_____

_____

_____

_____

_____

_____

_____

_____

Testing **Key Words**

A. Read the sentences below from "Preserving Native American Culture" on pages 49-50." Mark an X on the line next to the most important key words in each sentence. Then, on the lines provided, explain your choices.

1. "Well, if we Native Americans expect others to support our causes, we must educate people about our cultures."

   ____ Native Americans   ____ support

   ____ educate   ____ others

   _____

   _____

2. "When Native American culture is kept alive, the whole country is enriched."

   ____ Native American culture   ____ country

   ____ alive   ____ enriched

   _____

   _____

3. "It presented our beliefs regarding the earth, the family, and the purpose of art, among others."

   ____ presented   ____ beliefs

   ____ earth   ____ art

   _____

   _____

B. What role does art or the arts (including drama, music, dance) play in your culture? Write your response below and underline the key words that may help a reader better understand your ideas.

_____

_____

_____

_____

_____

Unit **FOUR**

BECOMING AN ACTIVE READER

Good readers of **editorials** are critical readers. They know that editorials are intended to persuade the reader. Good readers carefully evaluate each statement in an editorial and compare it with what they already know about the topic.

Using Skills and Strategies

Noting whether you are reading a **statement of fact** or **a statement of opinion** can help you read critically. You might ask: Which facts support the writer's position? Or, why has the writer included certain opinions? Do the facts and opinions support the writer's position?

Evaluating persuasive writing also can help you read critically. You might ask: How does the writer want me to think or behave? Does the writer's argument make sense to me? Has the writer convinced me? What in my own experience helps me to evaluate the writer's ideas?

In this unit, the skills of determining **fact and opinion** and **evaluating persuasive writing** will help you read critically.

Reading The Editorial

Reading editorials can help you clarify your position on an issue. People read editorials to find out the position of a school, a community, or a newspaper's general audience on an issue. Good readers do not automatically agree or disagree with the writer's viewpoint in an editorial. First they consider the facts and their own opinions.

Responding to Editorials

Remember to keep in mind your own experiences and opinions when reading editorials. Try jotting down your ideas as you read the editorials in this unit, "Stop Stereotyping Asians" and "Reasons for African Americans to Be Upbeat." Discuss your responses with your classmates.

Fact and Opinion

Lesson 7	Introducing *page 56*	Practicing *page 57*	Applying *page 58*	Reviewing *page 68*	Testing *page 69*

Introducing Strategies

In editorials, writers use **facts and opinions** to persuade readers to support their ideas. Good readers separate statements of fact—statements that can be proved—from statements of opinion—statements that make judgments. Distinguishing facts from opinions affects how readers respond to editorials. Readers might ask: Is the writer using this fact or opinion to persuade me to agree with his or her position? From my experience, do I agree or disagree with the statement?

The diagram below shows how readers think about statements of fact and statements of opinion when reading editorials.

QUESTION |||⟩	LOOK BACK |||⟩	RESPOND
What is the writer's position on the issue?	Can I find statements of fact and statements of opinion?	What are my responses to the facts and opinions?

Reading the Editorial

Read the editorial "Stop Stereotyping Asians" on pages 62-64 and the sidenotes on page 62. These sidenotes show how one good reader looked critically at facts and opinions while reading the editorial. After reading, complete the items below.

1. What are some facts and opinions that the reader identified?

_____

_____

2. Give one example of how the reader responded to the facts and opinions in the editorial.

_____

_____

_____

Practicing *Fact and Opinion*

A. Each opinion statement below is based on the editorial "Stop Stereotyping Asians." Circle the letter next to the fact that best supports each opinion. Then on the lines provided, explain the difference between the fact and the opinion.

1. Opinion Statement: Asian Americans have made outstanding contributions in the field of entertainment.
   a. "Star Trek" was the most popular TV series ever made.
   b. "Twin Peaks" was a very big hit.
   c. *The Great Wall* is a funny movie.
   d. George Takei played Lieutenant Sulu in *Star Trek* .

   _____

   _____

2. Opinion Statement: Kristi Yamaguchi was the shining star of the United States 1992 Olympic team.
   a. I think that skating is very good exercise.
   b. She won a gold medal at the Olympics.
   c. Millions of viewers prefer skating to baseball.
   d. She won the hearts of people all over the world.

   _____

   _____

3. Opinion Statement: Connie Chung is a very successful TV personality.
   a. She is the co-anchor on the "CBS Evening News."
   b. Everyone watches CBS.
   c. Young viewers prefer adventure programs.
   d. She is very pretty.

   _____

   _____

B. Write your opinion about something you feel strongly about. Then support your statement with two facts.

   Opinion: _____

   Fact: _____

   Fact: _____

Applying Fact and Opinion

A. Read the passage below. After you read it, answer the questions that follow.

LET'S STOP THE VIOLENCE NOW!

Something needs to be done soon to protect our children from exposure to murder and other violent acts shown routinely on television.

Experts have calculated that children will witness about 8,000 murders on TV before they finish elementary school. Since over 3,000 studies conducted over the years have shown that violence on TV begets violence in real life, TV violence must be taken seriously. We cannot sit back and accept the opinion of some experts who believe children understand violence on television is not real. Much of the violence occurs on Saturday morning cartoons, thought by many parents to be "safe" entertainment for their children. Children who see violence portrayed on television may indeed begin to think that acts of violence are "cool."

1. What is the writer's opinion about violence on television?

_____

_____

2. Look back at the passage and note two facts that support the writer's opinion.

_____

_____

B. Take a position on the issue of violence on television. Use at least two facts and two opinions to support your position.

_____

_____

_____

_____

To review
↓
page
68

_____

_____

_____

_____

Evaluating Persuasive Writing

Lesson 8	Introducing page 59	Practicing page 60	Applying page 61	Reviewing page 70	Testing page 71

Introducing Strategies

Unlike news articles, which basically give readers information, editorials are persuasive. Editorial writers use specific persuasive techniques to convince readers to agree with them. Persuasive techniques include telling stories, giving statistics, and using facts and opinions that appeal to reason or emotion. Good readers **evaluate persuasive writing** by asking questions such as: Why did the writer tell this story? Is he or she trying to appeal to my emotions so that it will change my mind? Are these statistics showing both sides of the issue?

The chart below shows how readers identify and evaluate persuasive techniques by reading critically.

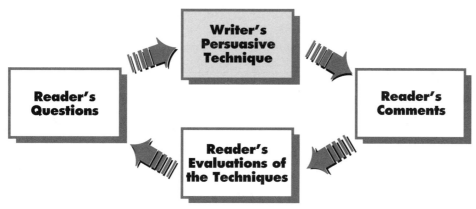

Reading the Editorial

Reread the article "Stop Stereotyping Asians" on pages 62-64. As you read, note which persuasive techniques the writer is using. After reading, complete the items below.

1. Does this writer use one basic technique or several techniques? Which one or ones?

_____

_____

2. Do you think the technique is effective? Why or why not? Use one example from the editorial to support your response.

_____

_____

Practicing *Evaluating Persuasive Writing*

A. Read each statement below about the editorial "Stop Stereotyping Asian Americans." Rewrite each statement correctly.

1. The writer of this editorial basically used the persuasive technique of storytelling.

_____

_____

2. To evaluate this editorial, the reader would have to think about whether the stories adequately support the writer's opinions.

_____

_____

3. Politics is one area where the writer suggests that Asian American participation might be decreasing.

_____

_____

4. The writer's argument is weakened because she includes no statistics to show that Asian American populations are growing in the United States.

_____

_____

B. Write a paragraph telling whether you think the writer's persuasive techniques were effective. Explain why you think the way you do. Use examples from the editorial to support your comments.

_____

_____

_____

_____

_____

_____

_____

Applying *Evaluating Persuasive Writing*

Read the passage below. After you read it, answer the questions that follow.

IMPOSE TEEN CURFEWS NOW!

Local officials, wake up! It's time to impose a 9 p.m. curfew on the youth of our town.

Three incidents during the past week prompt me to write this editorial. On Monday, around 10:30 p.m., Terry Williams of North Street missed a curve in the road and drove her parents' car into a ditch. On Friday night, town policemen caught five youths soaping the windows of cars parked along Main Street. On Saturday night, while walking home from a basketball game, John and Jim Clark were chased by a poodle. They might have been seriously hurt if Fifi hadn't been distracted by a cat. None of these events would have happened if these young people had been indoors after 9 p.m.

A curfew would have other benefits. Teens would have more time for homework. Their grades would improve. They could also help more with household chores. Because of all the benefits, let's give a curfew a try.

1. What position is the writer promoting?

_____

_____

2. What facts does the writer include to persuade readers to agree with the position?

_____

_____

_____

_____

3. Do you agree or disagree with the writer's position? Explain your own position below.

_____

_____

_____

To review

⬇

page
70

Dr. Woo is known worldwide as an author, artist, poet, and songwriter. She directs the Chinese Language Program at San Diego State University as well as its China Studies Institute. Dr. Woo's work has focused on helping people understand Chinese culture. In this editorial, she takes the position that Asian Americans are successful in all areas—not just in the sciences.

Stop Stereotyping Asians

by Catherine Yi-yu Cho Woo

The notes in the margins on this page show how one reader evaluated the facts and opinions presented in the editorial.

This editorial is about the issue of stereotyping Asian Americans. The writer's position is that they are successful in all areas, not just the sciences — I agree, based on my own observations —but let's see what the writer says.

These facts about Asian American winners of science prizes seem to support the stereotype. I guess she's presenting the other side of the issue here.

This paragraph is full of opinions. They are general statements, but she uses them to support her position.

Sometimes the writer backs up her position with facts and other times with a mix of facts and opinions. I think the words "shining star" and "won the hearts" make these statements convincing opinions.

It's a fact. Asian Americans *have* been very successful in the sciences. We have captured many Nobel prizes in these areas. Tsung-dao Lee and Chen Ning Yang won in physics (1986), and Yuan T. Lee (1986) and Samuel C. C. Ting (1976) in Chemistry. In 1993 Alfred Y. Cho became the first Chinese to receive the National Medal of Science, the highest honor that can be given to a scientist. Unfortunately, such outstanding achievements have led to a common, but faulty, belief that we Asian Americans *all* keep our faces glued to our computer screens. People tend to believe that we can work successfully only at scientific and technical subjects. This stereotype is reinforced when you study the make-up of schools of engineering around the country. For example, Asian Americans represented 49% of the 1991 freshman engineering class at UCLA and 50% of UC Berkeley's 1992 freshman engineering class.

But Asian Americans are as different from one another as the individuals in any other group. We each have different interests, different abilities, and different talents. You *can* find Asian Americans making their mark in the humanities and the social sciences. We are working and thriving among America's artists, musicians, writers, and actors; we are America's historians, politicians, and social critics. Let's look at some examples.

Asian Americans as athletes? Of course! Out on the ice, Kristi Yamaguchi was the shining star of America's 1992 Olympic team. She was a gold medalist who won the hearts of millions of viewers around the world. Michael Chang, a world-class tennis player and winner of the French Open, has come up against some of the greatest players in the world. Daring to go where few have gone before, the 30-member Korean Climbing Club of Los Angeles has tackled mountains around the globe. They have climbed every peak from El Capitan in the United States to Nameless Tower in the Himalayas.

Asian Americans also entertain us. Here are just a few of them. George Takei created the character of Lieutenant Sulu on the original "Star Trek" TV series. He then went on to play the same role in the *Star Trek* movies. Joan Chen starred in the movie *The Last Emperor* and was introduced to TV audiences in the hit series "Twin Peaks." On the other side of the camera we find director Peter Wong. He is perhaps best known for his comedy about how old China meets new China, *The Great Wall*.

In Los Angeles, an acting troupe known as the East West Players has been making gains in the entertainment industry since 1965. The group's goal is to blend Asian and American drama traditions. As Artistic Director Nobu McCarthy says: "We are still building Asian American-ness, and that comes first." Similar groups are located in San Francisco, Seattle, and New York City.

Of course, one of the most recognized faces in America, and a special favorite among young audiences, is Connie Chung. She's the nightly CBS News co-anchor. And I'm sure you've seen Ken Kashiwahara reporting from news hot spots around the world.

Many contributions to literature have been made by Asian Americans as well. David Henry Hwang's play *M. Butterfly* was a big hit on Broadway and won a Tony Award as Best Play in 1988. Playwright Philip Kan Gotanda is said to capture "the soul of Japanese America" in works like *Fish Head Soup*. In the field of fiction, Amy Tan has written about growing up as an Asian American. Her novels include the worldwide bestsellers *The Joy Luck Club* (1989) and *The Kitchen God's Wife* (1991).

On the music scene, the jazz group Hiroshima uses cultural influences from their Asian heritage—like the Japanese "guitar" or koto—in presenting their contemporary songs. Cellist Yo-yo Ma has brought new fans to classical music. He has even made appearances on the "Tonight Show." Seiji Ozawa is a classical conductor known throughout the world.

In architecture we find I.M. Pei and Minoru Yamasaki. Pei is known around the world for his creative and beautiful designs. Among them are the East Wing of the National Gallery in Washington, D.C., and the addition to the Louvre Museum in Paris, France. Painters, sculptors, and potters abound in the Asian American community. They offer unique ways of seeing the world we all share. And let's not forget the tasty contributions of the great Asian American chefs who add variety and spice to our menus!

Write your own sidenotes as you read the rest of the article. Identify statements of opinion and statements of fact. Tell whether or not you think the facts support the writer's opinions adequately.

Politics is another area in which the participation of Asian Americans has been steadily increasing. In the halls of Congress you might just bump into Senators Daniel Inouye and Daniel Akaka. Or you might run into Congressmen Robert Matsui and Norman Mineta. On the state level we find Governor Waihee in Hawaii and California Secretary of State March Fong Eu (who has served for more than 20 years in that office). A special case is that of California Assemblyman Nao Takasugi. The former city councilman and mayor of Oxnard, California, is also a survivor of the World War II internment camps. The fact that he was elected by a district with an Asian population of less than 7 percent shows the overwhelming support he had from non-Asian Americans. Across the country many more Asian Americans serve their local communities on boards, councils, and committees.

The example of Chang-Lin Tien, chancellor of UC Berkeley, makes it clear that Asian Americans don't have to choose between the sciences and other fields. Tien started out as an engineering student. He even worked for NASA, helping to build the space shuttles. Now he heads an important university and is interested in all types of education. As a student, he was even a basketball player!

Religion is one more area where Asian Americans are active. Grand Master Lin Yun is spiritual leader of the Black Sect of Tantric Buddhism and has a temple in Berkeley, California. He gives modern meaning to ancient wisdom, teaching ways to live in harmony with nature. The point of his lessons is to benefit our health, our wealth, our relationships with others, and our jobs. Master Lin Yun jets around the world, giving speeches and meeting with other religious leaders like the Pope and the Dalai Lama.

Asian Americans are the fastest growing minority in the United States. Chinese, Filipinos, Japanese, Indians, Koreans, Vietnamese—by the year 2050, our numbers are expected to increase by more than 400 percent. So, we can expect to see more and more Asian Americans lending their skills and talents to ever wider areas of interest. This will probably include the sciences, where they have been successful in the past. But we can also expect to see more and more Asian Americans in the arts, entertainment, politics, and social sciences.

So, please don't stereotype us. Asian Americans, like Americans from every heritage, can and do succeed in every field.

If you are working on

Lesson 7	Lesson 8
↓	↓
page 56	page 59

Donald E. Winbush is an Atlanta-based speechwriter, journalist, and creative writer. He is especially talented in creating brochures and other documents that promote businesses and their services in the African American community. This editorial suggests that African Americans are making strong gains in U.S. society.

There Are Lots of Reasons for African Americans to Be Upbeat

by Donald E. Winbush

As you read, make notes in the margins about how statements of fact and statements of opinion support the writer's position on the issue. Remember to include your responses in your notes.

The sky is falling! The sky is falling!

Remember that childhood story? An object fell on the head of Chicken Little. It came down with such force that Chicken Little believed the worst: the heavens were caving in. She decided to sound warnings.

Word spread quickly—as bad news often does. There was indeed a problem. But it was not nearly as bad as first thought. It turned out that the fallen object was not the sky, but a tiny acorn.

The sky is falling on the African American community—or so we are told. Cries of alarm are coming from all over: The African American family structure is crumbling. Teenage pregnancy rates in the African American community are at record levels. More African American men are under some form of restraint from the criminal justice system than are in college.

This is not an appeal to have these distressing signals ignored or dismissed. Obviously, serious problems do exist. Many have been thoroughly researched and documented. For example:

- The unemployment rate for African American men in the United States has not been less than 10 percent since 1979.

- More than 60 percent of African American households have annual incomes of less than $25,000.

- African American males are 6 percent of the general population but 47 percent of the prison population.

- More than 40 percent of African American children are growing up poor.

Yes, indeed, there are problems, and these problems are taking a heavy toll on the African American community.

But there is another concern: that we are emphasizing the problems too much. Stated another way, we are not emphasizing the positive enough. Sometimes, by dwelling on what is wrong, we lose sight of those things that are right. Without a balance, a distorted picture emerges.

There is a risk of this happening to the African American community. Problems can be stated so frequently and with such urgency that people have the impression that there is not much good news.

Nothing could be further from the truth. Of course African Americans are not a hopeless people. We are also not a helpless people.

Yet the possibility of such misleading images staying in people's minds increases every day. Positive accounts of African American life are smothered by negative news. An example of how that can occur is reflected in the following true story.

A young woman from the North who was visiting a friend in the South mentioned that she was surprised to find so many Southerners reading books. The Southerner was shocked to hear her friend make such an outrageous observation.

"Why in the world would you find that surprising?" the Southerner asked.

The Northerner replied, "I've always heard that illiteracy in the South is worse than in any other place in the country. I just didn't expect to find that many people with books."

What a distorted view! The influence of negative stories was so strong that the Northerner found some realities hard to imagine—like the fact that people from the South read books.

It is important that African Americans guard against that kind of narrow thinking being applied to them. In fact, not just African Americans should be concerned. One-dimensional thinking is harmful to everyone. Negative impressions bring negative responses.

How should we battle these distortions? Alex Haley, the author of *Roots,* had a personal motto that might apply here: "Find the good and praise it." Let's take a moment to do just that.

Despite the bleak statistics, people need not be

surprised that even in so-called "down-and-out" neighborhoods, solid African American businesses exist. Business owners are delivering courteous services and quality goods even as they struggle against great odds.

In those same neighborhoods, African American families are maintaining households. They are raising respectful children and sending them to college. Church, social, and civic organizations, such as fraternities, sororities, and block clubs, are organizing efforts to keep alive a sense of community.

Here are some statistics that are worth considering as seriously as those cited earlier:

- More than 40 percent of African Americans in this country are middle class and above.

- Between 1982 and 1987, the number of African American-owned businesses grew by nearly 38 percent—versus an overall 26 percent growth rate for U.S. businesses.

- Twelve percent of households headed by African Americans have incomes of $50,000 or more, up from 8 percent in 1980.

- More African Americans are enrolled in colleges and universities than at any other period in history.

The encouraging news does not have to stop here. Yet even these few facts serve to bring the picture of African American life into balance.

The time for finding the good in the African American community and praising it is now. As long as we fail to acknowledge the positives, we miss an opportunity to encourage more of the same.

If you are working on

Lesson 7	Lesson 8
↓	↓
page 68	page 70

Reviewing *Fact and Opinion*

A. Read the editorial "There Are Lots of Reasons for African Americans to Be Upbeat" on pages 65-67. As you read, circle statements of opinion and underline statements of fact. Write your responses in the margin. When you have finished, look over your notes. Select two statements from the editorial that you think were most effective in persuading you to agree with the writer. Use them to complete the diagram.

QUESTION	LOOK BACK	RESPOND
Writer's Position on the Issue	Statements of Fact and Statements of Opinion	My Responses

B. Do you agree or disagree with the writer's position on the topic? Write a paragraph stating your position. Use at least two facts and two opinions to support your position.

Testing *Fact and Opinion*

A. The paragraph below is based on the editorial "There Are Lots of Reasons for African Americans to Be Upbeat." As you read, fill in each blank with a word from the numbered list that makes the best sense.

It is the writer's _____ that people should learn
                              (1)
about the positive side of African American life, not just the

problems. In order to _____ this opinion, he notes
                              (2)
the advice of well-known African American Alex Haley. The

writer also provides some encouraging _____ about
                                              (3)
gains made by African Americans. He _____ not
                                          (4)
only African Americans, but all people, to avoid narrow

thinking and to acknowledge their accomplishments as well as

their problems. Has the writer of the editorial supported his

opinion well? In the final analysis, readers themselves will have

to decide if the writer's opinion is _____ or not.
                                            (5)

1. opinion
   detail

2. question
   support

3. facts
   problems

4. urges
   allows

5. humorous
   valid

B. Write an editorial. Take a position on an issue you are concerned about in your school. Use facts and opinions to support your position.

_____

_____

_____

_____

_____

_____

_____

_____

_____

_____

To begin
Lesson 8

page
59

Reviewing *Evaluating Persuasive Writing*

A. Reread the editorial "There Are Lots of Reasons for African Americans to Be Upbeat" on pages 65-67. As you read, identify phrases or sentences that illustrate the persuasive techniques used by the writer. Write some notes as you evaluate each technique. Use your notes to fill in the diagram below.

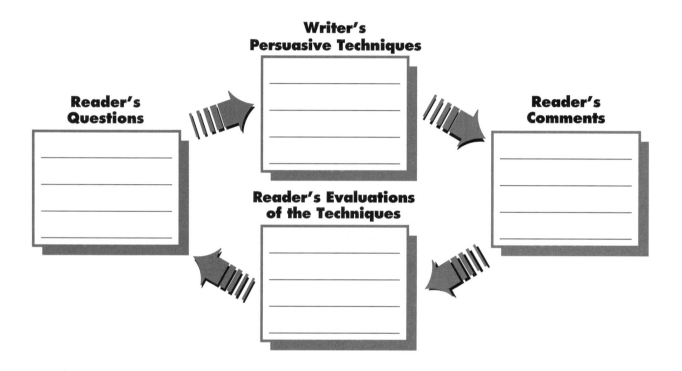

Writer's Persuasive Techniques

Reader's Questions

Reader's Comments

Reader's Evaluations of the Techniques

B. Write a paragraph explaining which technique used by the writer was the most effective. Use examples to support your response.

_____

_____

_____

_____

_____

_____

_____

_____

_____

Testing Evaluating Persuasive Writing

A. The incomplete statements below are based on the editorial "Reasons for African Americans to Be Upbeat" on pages 65-67. Mark an X in front of the phrase that best completes each statement. Then, on the lines provided, explain why you chose the answer you did.

1. The writer of the editorial takes the position that

    —— people should accentuate the positive side of African American life.

    —— statistics are very important in making your point.

    —— if you can't write anything good about people, then don't write anything at all.

    _____

    _____

2. In his editorial, the writer supports his position by

    —— noting statistics that give a more balanced view of African American life.

    —— comparing life in the North to life in the South.

    —— making readers feel guilty.

    _____

    _____

3. The writer tells the story about the Northerner's belief about Southern illiteracy to show that

    —— 12 percent of African American households have incomes of $50,000 or more.

    —— Southerners are better readers than Northerners.

    —— when negative news is everywhere, misleading images can distort the truth.

    _____

    _____

B. Another editorial writer might take the position that the serious problems in African American communities should be stressed so that solutions to them will be found. Write an editorial that takes this position. Use a separate piece of paper.

Unit FIVE

BECOMING AN ACTIVE READER

Good readers become actively involved when reading **plays**. To do this, they visualize the action, the setting, and the characters. They often feel as if they are a part of the characters' lives.

Using Skills and Strategies

The **plot** of a play consists of a series of events. As an involved reader, you might ask about the various elements in the plot: Which events make up the rising action? What is the conflict? What is the turning point, or climax? What happens in the falling action? What is the resolution?

You can also become involved in reading drama by identifying **pronouns** and the characters to which they refer. You might look back and ask: To which character does each pronoun refer? Is the reference clear?

In this unit, the skills of figuring out **plot** elements and identifying **pronoun** referents will help you read actively.

The Play: The Writer's Voice

Reading plays offers a unique opportunity to look into the lives of people across cultures. Stage directions help make the action, the setting, and the characters come alive. Natural dialogue can reflect the informal language of the characters. Reading plays actively can help readers break down cultural barriers and recognize similarities among all people.

Responding to Plays

It is important to jot down your responses as you read the plays in this unit, "A Change of Heart" and "Barbara Jordan: The Beauty Within Us." Write your notes in the side margins. Use them to discuss the plays with your classmates.

Plot

Introducing Strategies

Plot is the series of events that takes place in a story or play. Good readers pay attention to the plot by noticing what happens and the way it happens as the action unfolds. In drama, the plot begins with the rising action. As the action builds, a conflict, or a problem, is set up for one of the characters. The turning point of the play is called the climax. In the climax, the conflict reaches its highest point and the big plot question is answered. After the climax, the falling action leads to a resolution of the conflict.

The plot line below shows how readers can identify the important parts of a plot.

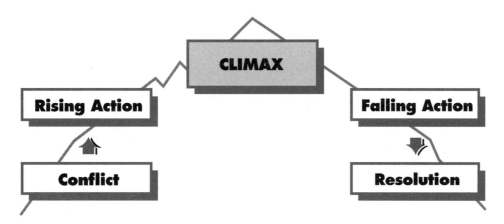

Reading the Play

Read "A Change of Heart" on pages 79-83. Use the play and the sidenotes on pages 79-81 to answer the questions below. The sidenotes show how one reader identified some important parts of the plot.

1. According to the reader, when does the rising action in the play begin?

_____

2. What conflict did the reader identify in the play?

_____

_____

Practicing *Plot*

A. The following statements are about the play "A Change of Heart." Circle the letter of the word or words that best complete each statement. Then on the lines provided, tell why you made each choice.

1. Part of the rising action in the play is when
   a. Greta and Darcy talk on the steps of the high school.
   b. Greta makes third string on the basketball team.
   c. Jeannine talks about chaperons at the dance.
   d. all of the above

   _____

   _____

2. The climax of the play comes when
   a. Greta sees Tyree walking by with Jeannine.
   b. Greta runs out of the gym.
   c. Greta calls Horace on the phone.
   d. none of the above

   _____

   _____

3. The resolution of the play is when
   a. Greta decides she wants to go to the dance with Tyree.
   b. Greta decides she likes Horace after all.
   c. Greta decides she doesn't like either boy.
   d. none of the above

   _____

   _____

B. Write a short paragraph describing your reaction to the resolution of the story. Did the resolution surprise you? In your opinion, was it a satisfactory resolution?

   _____

   _____

   _____

   _____

   _____

   _____

Applying *Plot*

Read the play excerpt below. Think about the plot line in the passage. Then answer the questions that follow.

CHARACTERS: ALBERTO: *a high school student*
VICTOR: *Alberto's friend*

SETTING: *The kitchen of Alberto's home*
VICTOR: (walking into the kitchen) *Hey, Alberto! My mom said you called and wanted to see me. What's going on?*
ALBERTO: (sitting at the table, algebra book in front of him) *Thanks for stopping by, Victor. Boy, did I have a rough day at school! First, Jenna said she wouldn't go to the dance with me. Then she said she couldn't come over to study. Now, I don't understand these algebra problems—and we have a test tomorrow!* (He picks up the book and slams it down on the table in frustration.)
VICTOR: (sitting down next to ALBERTO) *Calm down. Let me look at those problems.* (He pulls the book over to him.) *You know, I did really well in algebra last year. I'll bet I can explain these problems to you in no time. And who knows?*
ALBERTO: (laughing) *Maybe I'll even learn enough to pass that test tomorrow!*

1. What events are part of the rising action in the passage?

_____

_____

2. What is the conflict in the passage?

_____

_____

3. What is the resolution of the conflict?

_____

_____

To review
↓
page
90

Pronouns

Lesson 10	Introducing page 76	Practicing page 77	Applying page 78	Reviewing page 92	Testing page 93

Introducing Strategies

Pronouns are words such as *I, me, he, she, his, hers, us, you, yours, their, they* and *it* that take the place of nouns. Good readers look in the same sentence for the noun that the pronoun stands for. For example, in the sentence *Bob was supposed to meet Renee at the movies, but he never showed up,* the pronoun *he* refers to the noun *Bob.* A pronoun can also refer to a noun in a different sentence or even a different paragraph. To figure out which word a pronoun stands for, good readers look for gender, number agreement, and sentence clues.

The diagram below shows the process readers can use to identify the noun or pronoun to which a pronoun refers.

QUESTION	LOOK BACK	CIRCLE
What are some pronouns in the sentence? Are they singular or plural? Do they stand for a male or female?	To which noun does each pronoun refer? Does it agree in number and gender? Does it make sense?	Circle the noun to which each pronoun refers and draw a line between the words.

Reading the Play

Reread Greta's first words in Scene 1 of "A Change of Heart" on page 79. As you read, underline any pronouns. Then look back at Greta's words. Circle the nouns to which the pronouns refer and draw a line between them. After you have finished, complete the items below.

1. List two of the pronouns that you underlined in the scene and the nouns to which they refer.

_____

2. Tell how you decided on the correct nouns to circle.

_____

_____

Practicing *Pronouns*

A. Read the following passages from "A Change of Heart." Draw a line under the pronoun or pronouns in each passage. Circle the noun to which the pronoun or pronouns refer. Then on the lines provided, tell how you decided on the correct noun to circle.

1. (GRETA turns and rushes through the door. HORACE stands, hands outstretched, with a puzzled look on his face.)

_____

_____

2. (All girls except GRETA gather up their things and exit. MISS COLLINS sits down on the bleacher next to GRETA.)

_____

_____

3. JEANNINE: *(Laughing)* No problem. I just came to ask Auntie about this hunk who asked me to the dance.

_____

_____

4. AT RISE: GRETA enters, tosses her books on the coffee table, kicks off her shoes, and curls up on the sofa.

_____

_____

B. Write a paragraph that describes a conversation between two good friends. In your paragraph, use at least four pronouns.

_____

_____

_____

_____

_____

_____

_____

_____

Applying *Pronouns*

The following passage is an excerpt from the story "The Beautiful Girl of the Moon Tower." The story comes from the book *The People Could Fly: American Black Folktales* told by Virginia Hamilton. Read the passage and underline the pronouns. Then complete the items that follow.

> "... There was a son named Anton. He dreamed that a girl placed a handkerchief over his face. He woke up but he saw no one. Anton told his mother what he had dreamed. His mother said, "Anton, you've dreamed of something enchanted."
>
> A few days later Anton dreamed the dream again and it was exactly the same: A girl placed a handkerchief over his face.
>
> "Anton," his mother said, "you dream of a girl who lives with her father in the tower of the moon."
>
> Anton thought about how to get there, to the tower of the moon..."

1. What pronouns are used in the first paragraph of the excerpt? To what noun do those pronouns refer? How do you know?

_____

_____

_____

2. Reread the words that Anton's mother says. What two pronouns does she use? To what noun does each pronoun refer?

_____

_____

_____

3. The second paragraph in the excerpt uses the pronouns *it* and *his*. Rewrite the paragraph using the nouns to which those pronouns refer.

To review ⬇ page 92

_____

_____

_____

Darwin Walton believes that making a new friend can be more exciting than seeing a new movie or going on a wonderful trip. An African American writer, she has a special gift for writing conversations the way they are actually spoken. In this play, the exciting new friendship is a budding teenage romance.

A Change of Heart

by Darwin McBeth Walton

The notes in the margins on pages 79–81 show how one reader thought about the rising action, climax and resolution while reading the play, "A Change of Heart."

Characters

GRETA, a petite tenth-grader whose ambition is to be a star basketball player

DARCY, Greta's good friend and teammate

WYLENE, friend of Greta and Darcy

TYREE, eleventh-grade basketball star of Hickory High School

JEANNINE, new girl on campus, tall, good-looking

HORACE, studious, nice guy

MISS COLLINS, gym teacher and girls' basketball coach

◄ This list tells me who the characters are in the play and peaks my interest, but it doesn't say much about the plot. I'll read on to see what happens to the characters.

PLAY COMPLETE IN ONE ACT.

SCENE 1

SETTING: *Front steps of Hickory High School*

AT RISE: GRETA *and* DARCY *are sitting on the steps having a discussion.*

GRETA: No, you know darn well Tyree didn't ask me to the dance yet, but he did call last night. And guess what? He said he likes the gap between my teeth, that it made my eyes look bigger. He said he wanted to see me without my pony tail sometime.

◄ The action in this play starts to rise right away. I already know that Greta really likes Tyree and it sounds like she wants him to take her to the dance.

DARCY: *(Sarcastically)* I bet. So that's why you've got your hair down today.

GRETA: Hey, if that's what it takes! He said I'm his girl. And I do want to go to the dance with him. I'm meeting him here before class.

DARCY: I thought you said Horace asked you. What'd you tell him?

GRETA: That I wasn't sure I was going. (*Twirls her*

necklace nervously) And don't give me any business. Horace is not my type. Besides, Tyree asked me to go steady.

▶ DARCY: Girl, you're a trip. You know Tyree's tried to get every cute girl in school. You better get your act together and pay good old Horsey some attention. I think he's really stuck on you. You know he made the finals in the state poetry contest. Girl, suppose he wins that scholarship!

GRETA: I read about it. He said he wants to attend Tuskegee Institute. (*Looking up suddenly*) Oh, here comes Wylene. I heard she got an A on her science project.

DARCY: Yeah, she's Dr. Martin's pet pupil.

(WYLENE *approaches, and they all exchange greetings.*)

GRETA: Your hair looks great, Wy. Who did it for you?

WYLENE: (*Touching her black, curly hair*) You like it? I did it myself. (*Pause*) I hear you're going out for basketball again this year, Greta. You know, in tenth grade, we play the big girls. It ain't like the freshman team.

GRETA: I did okay last year. Made the first string, you know. (*Chews on necklace*)

WYLENE: I remember, but like I said, it's different from now on. Some of those girls are six feet tall. They'll clobber you. Well, don't say I didn't warn you. (*The bell rings. She turns and walks up the stairs.*)

▶ DARCY: Well, who asked her? Come on, girl, let's get to class. I'll see you at try. . . . (*She looks closely at* GRETA's *face.*) Girl, what's up? You look funny. (*She follows* GRETA's *stare and sees* TYREE *and* JEANNINE *coming up the walk.*) See, I've been trying to tell you.

GRETA: (*Recovering from her surprise and jealousy*) Walking with a girl doesn't mean anything. She's new and all the boys want to know a new girl. I know he's going to ask me to the dance today. You go ahead. I'll wait for him.

(DARCY *runs up the steps as* TYREE *and* JEANNINE *approach.* TYREE *looks at* GRETA *and waves, but continues up the steps with* JEANNINE. GRETA *stands stunned. Tears well up in her eyes. She turns and runs up the steps.*)

It sounds like Greta has a conflict here! She wants to be with Tyree, but Horace has asked her to the dance. Tyree doesn't sound like he's serious about her, but Horace does!

Here's something else that's adding to Greta's conflict. Tyree is walking with another girl! Maybe Greta should stick to Horace after all.

HORACE: (*Coming down the walk*) Hey, Greta, wait a minute!

(GRETA *does not wait. He catches up with her as she opens the door.*)

HORACE: Why are you rushing? The second bell didn't ring. (*Looking at her teary eyes*) Hey, what's the matter?

GRETA: Nothing. I just got something in my eye. What's up?

HORACE: I just wanted to know if you'd made up your mind about the dance.

GRETA: No. Well, yes. I mean, I don't think I can go. You'd better ask someone else.

HORACE: I don't want to ask anybody else. Why can't you go?

GRETA: I just can't. Now please leave me alone!

(GRETA *turns and rushes through the door.* HORACE *stands, hands outstretched, with a puzzled look on his face.*)

◀ The action is still rising at the end of this scene. The conflict hasn't reached its highest point yet. I'll read on to see what the climax of the play is. Then I'll look for the resolution to Greta's conflict.

Now write some of your own notes about the plot of the play. Write your notes in the margins. Look for the climax and how the conflict is resolved.

SCENE 2

SETTING: *Hickory High School gymnasium*

AT RISE: MISS COLLINS *is addressing a group of girls who are seated on the bleachers, dressed in basketball clothes. Among them are* GRETA, DARCY, *and* WYLENE.

MISS COLLINS: Now, I know some of you sophomores are disappointed. But you're still growing and getting better. We'll play intramurals, just like always. You'll get your chance to play. Class dismissed. (*She looks at* GRETA *and speaks quietly to her.*) Greta, see me after class.

(*All girls except* GRETA *gather up their things and exit.* MISS COLLINS *sits down on the bleacher next to* GRETA.)

GRETA: Yes, Miss Collins?

MISS COLLINS: Cheer up. You made third string. You'll get to play. Not as much as you did last year, but you'll play. You're up against some tough competition now, and you'll do just fine. When you're a junior. . . . (JEANNINE *walks up.*) Oh, hello, Jeannine. Are you getting to know everyone? Have you met Greta? Greta, this is my niece, Jeannine Turner from New York City.

JEANNINE: Yeah, we've met. Hi, Greta.

GRETA: Hi. (*Making an effort to be friendly*) How do you like our school?

JEANNINE: It's different but I do like it here. (*Pause*) Auntie, will you be at the dance Friday night?

MS. COLLINS: I've been asked to chaperone. (*Walks offstage*)

JEANNINE: Chaperone? How nerdy! (*She looks at GRETA.*) You mean you all need to be chaperoned?

GRETA: We *all* don't need to be, but it's a school rule. Some faculty members are at all school functions. Surely that's not news to you.

JEANNINE: Hey, lighten up! Just kidding! They have armed *police* patrols at school functions where I come from.

GRETA: Sorry. I guess I'm kinda short-tempered today.

JEANNINE: (*Laughing*) No problem. I just came to ask Auntie about this guy who asked me to the dance. Maybe you know him—Tyree? He's too good-looking to trust. You know anything about him?

GRETA: Well, uh, not much. But you're probably right not to trust him. He's pretty slick.

JEANNINE: Slick? Girl, this guy makes an oil spill look like a sandbox. Of course, I can handle him. I just wanted to check him out, see if he's worth my time. Is he dating anybody steady? I don't want to make any enemies over some fool who thinks he's Mr. Wonderful.

GRETA: I'm sure you'll work it out. (*Abruptly*) I've gotta go. See you around. (*She turns and runs out of the gym.*)

SCENE 3

SETTING: *Sidewalk outside the gymnasium.*

AT RISE: DARCY *is waiting for* GRETA, *who comes barreling down the sidewalk as the scene opens, nearly running into* DARCY.

DARCY: Girl, you look like you lost your last
friend. How'd you do? I made second team. (*She
hands* GRETA *a sealed envelope.*) Horsey asked
me to give this to you. It looks important. Open it,
open it!

GRETA: What's he up to now? I told him I wouldn't go to
the dance with him. Doesn't he know what "no"
means? (*She rips the envelope open, takes out a sheet
of folded paper, and smoothes it out.*)

DARCY: (*Reading over* GRETA's *shoulder*)

> Greta, who brings out the greatness in me,
> Makes me aware of possibilities,
> Of things I never expected to see,
> In a man I never expected to be.

Hey, girlfriend, that's good! What's with you?

GRETA: Get real! (*She folds up the sheet.*)

DARCY: Aw, Greta, c'mon! Read the rest of it.

GRETA: (*Breathes deeply and groans*) Oh, all right! But,
Darcy, if you breathe a word of this to anybody,
you're dead! (*She continues reading the poem.*)

> Oh, Greta, be for me all I dream you can be;
> My sun, my sky, my deep blue sea,
> My day, my night, my unfailing star.
> Be for me, Greta, all that you are.

This is real hoaxie! Is he serious?

DARCY: He's serious. Hey, I think it's romantic! Nobody
ever wrote a love poem to me. I'm jealous. Keep
reading, girl.

GRETA: (*Continuing to read*)

> Be my joy and my sorrow,
> My reason for tomorrow,
> And, at my insistence,
> My reason for existence.
> Be my star, and all that you ever are.

That's it. That's enough. I'm not reading another word.
I'm going home. I'll see you tomorrow. (*She walks
off.*)

DARCY: 'Bye, girlfriend. Don't you throw that poem away.
Good old Horsey may be famous one day. It'll be
worth some mon-ee! (*Exits in other direction*)

SCENE 4

SETTING: GRETA'*s living room.*

AT RISE: GRETA *enters, tosses her books on the coffee table, kicks off her shoes, and curls up on the sofa.*

GRETA: (*Takes out the poem and reads the last verse in a soft dreamy voice*)

> You are my song,
> So that I'm never alone.
> Greta, please always recall
> You are my love, my life, my all.

(*Twirling her necklace, she gazes thoughtfully into the distance. Then she picks up the telephone and dials a number.*)

GRETA: (*In a sweet voice*) Hello, Horsey—I mean, Horace?

CURTAIN

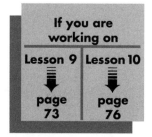

If you are
working on

Lesson 9	Lesson 10
⬇	⬇
page 73	page 76

Brenda Lane Richardson is the author of *Story Power: Talking to Teens in Turbulent Times*. Her concern about teenagers is but one quality that she shares with Barbara Jordan—her eloquence and her African American heritage are others. Barbara Jordan, the main character in Richardson's one-act play, served in the U.S. House of Representatives from 1972 until 1978. Although the following scene never actually took place, Jordan did campaign for President John Kennedy and Vice President Lyndon B. Johnson. Johnson is known to have thought highly of Congresswoman Jordan. Many of their words in this drama are taken from their speeches.

Barbara Jordan: The Beauty Within Us

by Brenda Lane Richardson

Write your own sidenotes as you read. Focus on the plot of the play, especially the conflict, the climax, and the resolution. Use the wide margins for your notes.

Characters

BARBARA JORDAN, a 24-year-old woman

ALMA, a fellow campaign worker, about 19 years old

BETTY, a fellow campaign worker, about 23 years old

LYNDON JOHNSON, a middle-aged Southerner in glasses and cowboy hat

A ONE-ACT PLAY

TIME: *Friday evening, Autumn 1959*

SETTING: *A Democratic campaign office in Houston, Texas*

AT RISE: *Stacks of paper overflow from baskets that sit on two well-worn desks. The walls are covered in large hand-lettered signs that read "Vote Kennedy-Johnson 4 A Change."*

As the lights brighten, BARBARA can be seen at a desk covered with books. She moves from book to book, looking up information and mouthing unfamiliar words.

When not rushing to the window to search impatiently for someone, BETTY is pacing the floor.

ALMA, who is seated, wears a campaign hat. In her impatience, she drums her fingers on the desk.

Although BARBARA continues reading, both BETTY and ALMA freeze when a voice is heard over the loud speaker.

VOICE: Attention. We have just received word that our vice presidential candidate, Lyndon B. Johnson, will not be visiting us as scheduled. We are sorry to disappoint you. Please turn the lights out in each of the offices before you leave.

ALMA: (*Pulling off her hat and tossing it onto the desk as she stands*) All this waiting for nothing.

BETTY: We could be at the party.

ALMA and BETTY: Bobby, you haven't heard a word that has been said. Ol' Lyndon has canceled on us. He's busy with the big shots. Let's go to the party.

BARBARA: (*Returning to her books, she mumbles.*) Perhaps we shall see him on another occasion.

BETTY: (*Walking to Barbara's desk and gently taking the book from her*) You're always reading. It's time to dance.

ALMA: Everyone knows how smart you are. Enough with the books!

BARBARA: A genius or a donkey. No one will know the difference if I'm not prepared. You two should stay and find out more about these two men we're working for.

ALMA: I already know what I need to. Kennedy's cute, and Johnson's a charmer.

BARBARA: That's not going to help them win. I don't know about you, but I do not intend to support losers. I'd rather devote my full attention to figuring out how I can help them and, at the same time, help our people.

(*Laughing loudly, BETTY and ALMA exit, waving goodbye. There are a few seconds of silence as BARBARA continues reading. Suddenly, the lights go out and we hear BARBARA gasp. A voice can be heard over the loudspeaker.*)

VOICE: Attention. We are experiencing a momentary power failure. In the meantime, we will send a janitor around to check each office.

(*Seconds later, a door can be heard opening and shutting.*)

BARBARA: Hello. Is someone there?

JOHNSON: (*In a booming voice*) Well, ain't this a pretty can of worms.

BARBARA: You needn't worry about checking me.

JOHNSON: So, a young lady who's not afraid of the dark and a stranger.

BARBARA: Perhaps I will be when I look back on this episode. But I'm not someone who worries about the past. I'd much prefer to concentrate on the now. And right now, I'm fine.

JOHNSON: You sure do have a pretty voice. . . . I bet if God were a woman, she'd sound just like you.

BARBARA: That's one of the most gracious compliments I've ever received. Thank you. But shouldn't you be checking the fuse box or something?

JOHNSON: Actually, I prefer to rest my doggies. I've been on 'em all day. (*He can be heard searching for a chair and sitting.*) So what's a nice little lady like you doing here on a Friday night?

BARBARA: Reading, actually.

JOHNSON: Student?

BARBARA: Not any longer.

JOHNSON: (*Eagerly*) Where'd you go to school?

BARBARA: Most recently, Boston University's School of Law.

JOHNSON: Did you know that Rockefeller lad up there?

BARBARA: I can't say I knew him.

JOHNSON: I bet we know a lot of the same people. So now tell me again. Why are you reading in a campaign office on a Friday night?

BARBARA: I was waiting for our vice presidential candidate.

JOHNSON: Why, that's m . . .

BARBARA: Unfortunately, he's living up to his reputation of being unpredictable.

JOHNSON: (*Sounding insulted and amused*) You don't say. I mean, do folks really say that? (*When she doesn't respond, he continues.*) Why would you work for someone who can't be where he says he's going to be?

BARBARA: Because I believe Kennedy and Johnson care about young people and will offer us opportunities to have a voice in the government. I also believe they will engineer the changes that this state and this country so desperately need.

JOHNSON: I couldn'ta said it better myself. . . . Kennedy and I, I mean and that fellow Johnson, aren't promising to change folks' lives, but at least they can change their opportunities.

BARBARA: I believe that. I have to. I look around at the squalor and poverty and the injustice in this country and I pray that someone will end human suffering.

JOHNSON: I wish I could see you. What do you look like?

BARBARA: Something like an old face you might pass any day.

JOHNSON: Oh, come on . . .

BARBARA: No, you misunderstand. I may not be an exotic flower that stops people in their tracks. But as long as God's good sunlight shines down, I can grow as high as I wish.

JOHNSON: I can almost picture you from your voice. Are you blonde or brunette? Freckles or none?

BARBARA: (*She laughs.*) I have one freckle on my ear. Does that count? But wait. I can picture you, too. Are you wearing a janitor's uniform? Do you have tools in your belt?

(*Suddenly, the lights come on. They stare open-mouthed at each other.*)

BARBARA: Why, you're . . .

JOHNSON: (*Also staring*) And you're . . . (*He takes off his hat, bowing slightly*) Pleased to meet ya' ma'am.

BARBARA: I'm sure I don't look at all as you'd expected.

JOHNSON: You're right about that. But I'll tell you one thing, I've used the word beautiful many times in my life, but I didn't know what that meant, . . . until now.

BARBARA: How can you possibly say that?

JOHNSON: I've known a lot of women in my time, some all fancy out front but as empty inside as a chicken house after the fox visits, if you know what I mean. Let me just tell you this. Your words and your intelligence bathe you in such a flattering light, any young man would be honored to know you.

BARBARA: Do you sincerely believe that?

JOHNSON: Every bit as much as I believe Jack Kennedy will be president and as much as I know I'll get to invite you to the White House. Would you be kind enough to leave me your name and address?

BARBARA: (*She writes quickly, then gathers her books.*) Then we will meet again, in Washington. Right now, I've got to run. (*She holds her head high.*) I have a dance to go to.

(*After she exits, the voice from the loud speaker can be heard.*)

VOICE: Attention. I have been informed that our vice presidential candidate is approaching the building. . . . Hello, . . . Hello. Is anybody there?

(*JOHNSON exits the stage, and the lights darken.*)

If you are working on

Lesson 9	Lesson 10
↓	↓
page 90	page 92

Reviewing *Plot*

A. Read the play "Barbara Jordan: The Beauty Within Us" on pages 85-89. As you read, think about the plot of the play. Use the plot line below to list the important parts of the plot.

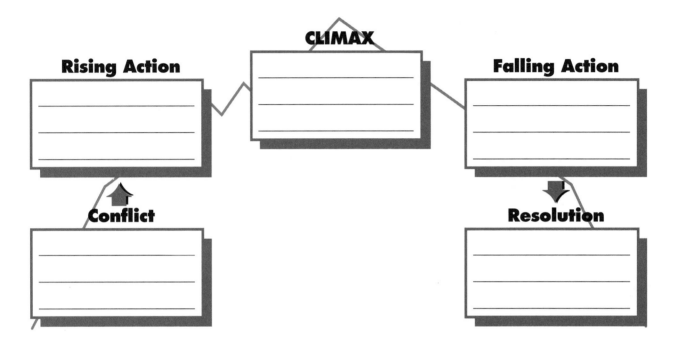

CLIMAX

Rising Action

Falling Action

Conflict

Resolution

B. Imagine that you are Barbara Jordan. In her words, explain the significance of Lyndon Johnson's visit. Tell how the visit changed the way that Barbara felt about herself.

_____

_____

_____

_____

_____

_____

_____

_____

_____

_____

Testing *Plot*

A. Fill in the circle next to the words that best completes each statement about the play "Barbara Jordan: The Beauty Within Us." On the line provided, tell why you chose that response.

1. When Alma and Betty tried to get Barbara to go to the party, their actions were
   ○ part of the rising action in the play.
   ○ part of the falling action in the play.
   ○ the climax of the play.
   ○ the resolution of the play.

   _____

2. Barbara's refusal to go to the dance reflects
   ○ the climax of the play.
   ○ the conflict in the play.
   ○ the falling action of the play.
   ○ the resolution of the play.

   _____

3. The lights going on signal
   ○ the rising action in the play.
   ○ the falling action in the play.
   ○ the climax of the play.
   ○ the resolution of the play.

   _____

4. Barbara's words "I have a dance to go to" reflect
   ○ the climax of the play.
   ○ the conflict in the play.
   ○ the rising action in the play.
   ○ the resolution of the play.

   _____

B. What do you think would have happened if the lights had not gone out? How might that have affected the resolution of Barbara's conflict? Write a paragraph in which you give your opinion. Make notes here.

To begin
Lesson 10

page
76

_____

_____

Lesson 10	Introducing *page 76*	Practicing *page 77*	Applying *page 78*	Reviewing *page 92*	Testing *page 93*

Reviewing Pronouns

A. Reread the introduction to the play about Barbara Jordan on page 85. Look for pronouns as you read. Then use the diagram below to help you identify the noun to which each pronoun refers.

QUESTION	LOOK BACK	CIRCLE
What are some pronouns in the sentence? ________________ ________________ Are they singular or plural? ________________ Do they stand for a male or female? ________________ ________________	To which noun does each pronoun refer? ________________ ________________ Does it agree in number? ________________ Does it agree in gender? ________________ Does it make sense? ________________	Circle the noun to which each pronoun refers. Draw a line between the words.

B. Look at the pronouns that you wrote in the blanks. Use as many of the pronouns as possible in a paragraph of your own. You might wish to write about an election in your own school.

Testing *Pronouns*

A. The following passage can be completed using pronouns. Read the passage and fill in each blank with a pronoun that makes sense within the context of the sentences.

The presidential candidate stepped up to the podium. The crowd roared and applauded wildly. Then the candidate held up _____ arms, and the crowd quieted. The candidate began to speak. _____ voice was firm and sincere.

"Thank you so much!" said the candidate. Without _____ support, this never would have happened. _____ would also like to thank Betty. _____ dear wife has been understanding and devoted. Without _____ by my side, today would only be a dream!

Then the candidate stepped away from the podium. Walking around _____, the candidate moved to the edge of the stage. Again the crowd yelled and clapped. "With _____ help," said the candidate, "the election will be won!" In the next four years, life for _____ and _____ children can only get better and better!"

B. Write your impression of a current political leader. Use pronouns in your description. Then let a partner read your writing. Can your partner identify the noun to which each pronoun refers?

_____

_____

_____

_____

Unit *SIX*

BECOMING AN ACTIVE READER

Good readers are active readers. As they read **plays,** they stay involved by predicting what will happen next. They compare their own experiences and feelings to those presented by the characters.

Using Skills and Strategies

Asking what will happen next or **predicting outcomes** will help you read actively. You might ask: What is happening at the beginning? Based on my own experiences and story events, what will probably happen next? What will be the outcome at the end of the story?

Identifying **problems** helps you get involved in a play. You might ask: What problems do the characters face? What events take place as a result of the problems? Are the problems **solved** at the end of the play?

In this unit, the skills of **predicting outcomes** and identifying **problems** and **solutions** will help you read plays actively.

Reading the Play

In a play, the text is divided into speeches. These speeches, or the words each character says, carry the action or plot. Stage directions, usually in italic type, give the reader descriptions of actions and the setting. Paying close attention to how dialogue, setting and plot are treated can help you read plays actively and stay involved.

Responding to Plays

Good readers usually respond to the characters in a play through the dialogue and the stage directions. It is important to write down your responses to the characters' words and actions as you read "The Strange Case of My Brother, or the Saturday Mystery" and "The Heritage Project." Share these ideas as you discuss the plays.

Predicting Outcomes

Introducing Strategies

Good readers often think about what will happen next or what the outcome will be as they read a play or story. To **predict outcomes,** readers relate clues from the story to their own experiences and make guesses about what will happen next. Their predictions may or may not reflect what actually happens. Therefore, good readers adjust their predictions as the action unfolds.

The chart below shows how one good reader used story clues as well as personal experiences to make predictions while reading a play.

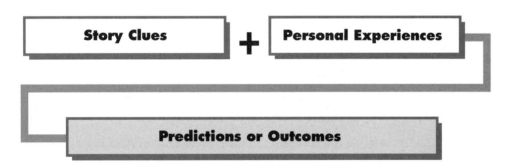

Reading the Play

Read "The Strange Case of My Brother, or The Saturday Mystery" on pages 101–108 and the sidenotes on page 101–102. These notes show how one good reader used story clues and personal experiences to predict outcomes. Then answer the questions below.

1. What does the reader think the play will be about?

_____

_____

2. List some of the clues the reader notes that might be important in figuring out what's going to happen.

_____

_____

_____

Practicing *Predicting Outcomes*

A. The incomplete statements below are based on the play "The Strange Case of My Brother, or the Saturday Mystery" on pages 101-108. Circle the letter next to the words that best complete each statement. Then on the line that follows, explain your answer.

1. When Kelsie asks Jamar what he is doing at 5:30 A.M. with the family bank, the reader might make a prediction based on the fact that
   a. Kelsie and Jamar seem to be close.
   b. the family seems to work hard together.
   c. the hiding place is known to everyone.
   d. all of the above.

   _____

2. When Donnie explains that he saw Jamar go inside a lit up abandoned house before dawn, the reader might predict that
   a. Donnie will follow Jamar.
   b. Donnie will call the police.
   c. Donnie will support his friend.
   d. none of the above.

   _____

3. When Donnie, Cassandra, and Kelsie see Jamar inside the abandoned house and hear music playing in the background, the reader might predict that
   a. Jamar has just helped out a family in need.
   b. the friends are upset because they weren't invited to the party.
   c. Kelsie will now help out whoever lives in this abandoned house.
   d. Jamar is doing something he shouldn't be doing.

   _____

B. What would you think if you discovered a family member awake at an early hour in the kitchen? What would you say or do in that situation? Write your response in two or three sentences below.

_____

_____

_____

Applying *Predicting Outcomes*

A. Read the scene below from a play. Then answer the questions that follow.

(Suretta and Carl are waiting at 3 P.M. for the school bus)

SURETTA: *It's so cold. That bus better get here soon. I mean soon!*

CARL: *I only have a minute or two left.*

SURETTA: *What do you mean, Carl? Where are you going besides home? (She looks surprised.)*

CARL: *I've got someplace to go, that's all. It's important they think I got on the school bus.*

SURETTA: *Carl, what are you up to?*

CARL: *Did you see that advertisement in the local paper about the job at the movie theater downtown?*

SURETTA: *(Hesitating while trying to remember) Right. That's right.*

CARL: *(a smile creeps across his face) Well... (the school bus turns the corner and pulls up)*

1. What do you predict might happen next in this scene?

_____

_____

2. What is one story clue that helped you make your prediction?

_____

_____

3. What about your personal experience helped you make your prediction?

_____

_____

B. Think of a situation for which someone could predict an outcome. Write it in two or three sentences below. Ask a classmate to predict an outcome for the situation. Then discuss how the prediction was made.

To review

↓

page
115

_____

_____

_____

Problem and Solution

Introducing Strategies

Authors create characters in plays and stories that usually have a problem to solve. Finding **solutions** to the **problems** often create the plot, or series of events. The turning point occurs in the plot when it appears that a solution has been found. Good readers become involved in fiction by noting the characters' problems, events that lead to a solution, and the turning point.

The chart below can help guide you as you identify the character's problem, the events that lead to a solution, the turning point, and the eventual solution.

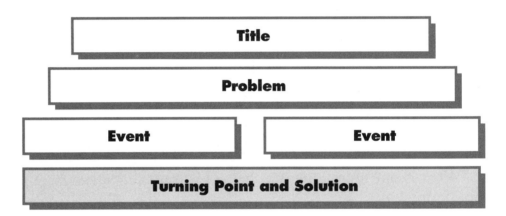

Title

Problem

Event   **Event**

Turning Point and Solution

Reading the Play

Reread the play "The Strange Case of My Brother, or The Saturday Mystery" on pages 101-108. As you read, underline details that tell the characters' problems, the turning point, and events that lead to a solution. Then answer the questions that follow.

1. What is the major problem in the play?

_____

2. When does the turning point happen?

_____

3. What is the solution to the problem?

_____

Practicing **Problem and Solution**

A. The incomplete sentences below are based on the play "The Strange Case of My Brother, or The Saturday Mystery" on pages 101-108. Circle the letter next to the word or phrase that best completes each statement. Then on the lines provided, relate the statement to the problem, the turning point, and the solution.

1. At the beginning of the play, Kelsie finds Jamar in the
   a. kitchen.   b. Weaver house.   c. jogging park.

   _____

   _____

2. Kelsie believes that Jamar got the money by
   a. begging.   b. working.   c. stealing.

   _____

   _____

3. At 5:30 A.M., after Kelsie and Jamar speak, Jamar
   a. leaves the house.   c. puts money in the bank.
   b. goes back to sleep.

   _____

   _____

4. Donnie, Cassandra, and Kelsie decide to go out and visit
   a. their school.   c. the Weaver house.
   b. the jogging park.

   _____

   _____

B. In your own words, describe the major problem in the play and how it was solved. Use details from the play in your description.

   _____

   _____

   _____

   _____

   _____

Applying *Problem and Solution*

A. Read the excerpt below from a play. Then answer the questions that follow.

(Sitting around a table in the kitchen after school)

AMY: *What's up, Tim? You look puzzled.*

TIM: *How would you find out about the way of life in two different geographic regions in the world? That's my geography assignment for this week.*

AMY: *You mean—like life in the desert and life on the tundra?*

TIM: *That's it exactly.*

AMY: *Here's a thought, Tim. Mom and Dad are hosts for their travel club tomorrow night. You can talk to Mr. and Mrs. Wilson.*

TIM: *Why them?*

AMY: *They're from Alaska. And the Murak family lived in Egypt for two years.*

TIM: *Egypt, home of the Sahara! What would I do without a brilliant older sister like you?*

1. What problem is presented in this excerpt?

_____

_____

2. What is the turning point for the characters as they try to solve the problem?

_____

_____

3. What is the solution to the problem?

_____

_____

B. How could Tim have solved his problem if his parents had not been in a travel club? Suggest a possible solution on the lines below.

To review
page 117

_____

_____

_____

_____

_____

Jerdine Nolen Harold lives in Baltimore, where she writes and teaches. She has won many awards, including a Black History grant and a folk tales-writing grant. This play reflects her African American heritage and the pride she takes in encouraging students to become effective problem-solvers.

The Strange Case of My Brother, or The Saturday Mystery

by Jerdine Nolen Harold

The notes in the margin show how one good reader used story clues and personal experience to predict the outcome of the play.

Characters

KELSIE, *a 10th grader*

JAMAR, *her fraternal twin brother*

DONNIE,CASSANDRA, *Kelsie and Jamar's friends and classmates*

PLAY COMPLETE IN ONE ACT.

SCENE 1: *The kitchen at KELSIE'S and JAMAR'S house. It is early morning, close to daybreak.*

◄ Jamar and Kelsie are awake very early. This probably means something unusual is happening.

AT RISE: *The house is quiet. The household is asleep, except for JAMAR, who enters stage right. He tiptoes to a cabinet and takes out a canister that serves as the family piggy bank. He counts out a number of bills, and tries to conceal them in his fist as he hears someone entering the room. It is his sister, KELSIE.*

◄ Why is Jamar taking money from the family bank? Is Kelsie right? There must be other clues in the play to help me predict what will happen next.

KELSIE: *(Surprised, shocked, even outraged by what she sees her brother doing)* Jamar, what are you doing with the *family* bank?

JAMAR: *(Angrily)* None of your business. Go back to bed. And don't talk so loud. You want to wake up Mom and Dad?

◄ This family seems close—they're saving money in a bank—like on an honor system—and the children seem to have a good relationship. What's happening is unusual, but I predict nothing bad will happen.

KELSIE: *(In a whispered, yet angry tone)* Maybe I do! And it *is* my business. What's that you've got balled up in your hand? If it's what I think it is, it belongs to the family.

The Strange Case of My Brother, or The Saturday Mystery ■ **101**

JAMAR: What's that supposed to mean?

KELSIE: You know, *(she whispers)* stealing . . .

Jamar doesn't seem to be a trouble maker, so I don't think he's causing trouble now. Maybe he's got a secret plan for the money. Is he going to do something good with it?

▶ JAMAR: *(Breaking in)* I don't steal. I took what's mine, my part.

KELSIE: Yeah, but that's just it, you're *taking* it. You didn't tell me about it. What about cluing me in on this? I'm your sister, remember. Your *twin* sister!

JAMAR: *(Brushing her off)* Kelsie, this doesn't have anything to do with you. You just stay out of this. Besides, I'll have the money back in there this evening, when I get my paycheck.

Jamar's friends might provide more clues in Scene 2. I predict a good outcome—but what it'll be, though, I'm not sure of just yet.

▶ KELSIE: Boy, don't play with me! Why are you so secretive all of a sudden? What's going on? Where do you go at night? What do you do? Why are you sneaking things out of the house without telling me? You're not doing dr . . .

Now make some of your own predictions as you read. Remember to use story details and personal experiences. Write your notes in the margins.

JAMAR: *(Interrupts abruptly)* No. And I'm not secretive all of a sudden. Besides, you wouldn't understand.

KELSIE: Jamar, how could you say that? This is *me* you're talking to!

JAMAR: *(He looks earnestly at his sister, trying to recapture her trust. He wants to say something, use the right words to make her understand, but he is unable.)* Kelsie . . .

KELSIE: What is it, Jamar? You can tell me!

JAMAR: Kelsie *(he starts, then pauses)* . . . Never mind. I gotta go. It will be light soon. *(He moves toward the door.)*

KELSIE: *(Looking at the kitchen clock)* Of course it's gonna be light soon. It's 5:30 A.M. *(She looks surprised.)* What am I supposed to tell Mom and Dad if they wake up? *(Jamar puts his hand on the knob of the back door.)* Wait a minute! This is supposed to be our Mystery Saturday for English class. Remember? This is our last weekend to get ready with Donnie and Cassandra. The project's due on Monday. Remember?

JAMAR: (Sounding a bit rushed) Yeah, well, I have to cancel. Do it without me, okay? I'll catch up with you later. You'll fill me in.

KELSIE: No, Jamar. We need you!

JAMAR: (Sounding exasperated) You'll do just fine without me. (Now in a more jovial tone) Go back to bed, little girl!

KELSIE: (Acknowledging her brother's attempt at humor) You don't look so good.

JAMAR: (Teasing and clutching his throat) Don't tell me I look pale.

KELSIE: Well, you do. . . .

JAMAR: I have never looked pale in this skin. (He is stretching the joke. It is apparent that he is trying to humor his sister before he leaves.)

KELSIE: (Very concerned) Jamar? (She is pleading now, reaching for his hand.)

JAMAR: (Returning to his previous abruptness) Leave me alone. I told you I don't like it when you do that. Besides, I gotta get out of here!

(JAMAR exits through the back door into the ribbon of morning. KELSIE watches him through the kitchen window.)

SCENE 2: Still in the kitchen, later that same morning.

AT RISE: KELSIE is standing at the kitchen sink. She is finishing the dishes from breakfast. She turns the water off, cocking her head as if listening. There is a knock at the back door that ends when she turns off the water.

KELSIE: Donnie? Cassandra? Is that you?

(There is no answer.)

KELSIE: (More insistently) Donnie? Cassandra? If that is you, answer me!

(After a long silence, the door opens slowly, creaking mysteriously. DONNIE and CASSANDRA enter quickly and briskly. DONNIE'S coat is caped over his shoulder. His hat is turned so that the brim is sideways. He is moving quickly about the room while CASSANDRA, holding a magnifying glass, examines objects closely.)

DONNIE: *(Using a British accent, like Sherlock Holmes)* Elementary, my dear Cassandra, elementary!

CASSANDRA: Holmes, you've done it again! *(She applauds as DONNIE takes a bow.)*

KELSIE: *(Obviously irritated)* Stop it right now! I've had enough mystery for one day!

CASSANDRA: *(Shocked by KELSIE'S tone)* Girl, what is wrong with you? We're just having some fun, trying to crack you up. . . .

KELSIE: *(Apologetically)* I'm sorry. I'm just so upset with Jamar.

DONNIE: *(Acting heroic)* What did he do to my girl now? Are your parents here?

(KELSIE shakes her head no.)

DONNIE: *(Changing roles quickly. He shrugs off his "cape" and rips the hat off his head.)* Hey, Jamar! *(He uses a loud, tough-guy voice.)* Man, get in here! *(Now he shadow-boxes.)*

KELSIE: *(With a big sigh)* Forget it. He's not here either.

CASSANDRA: *(Somewhat shocked)* Not here? Well, when's he coming back?

KELSIE: *(Shaking her head)* I don't know. He left here at 5:00 A.M. this morning.

DONNIE: *(Soothingly)* What's wrong with that? He probably had some business to take care of. He should be walking in any time now.

KELSIE: *(Irritated and upset)* I don't know. I caught him taking money out of the family bank.

CASSANDRA: *(Shocked)* Stealing?

KELSIE: *(Dismayed)* He said he'd return it this evening after he got off work.

CASSANDRA: Don't you believe him?

KELSIE: I don't know what to believe. It's like I don't even know who he is anymore. He has changed. He seems preoccupied all the time. He leaves the house at all kinds of weird hours and doesn't let my parents know. I'm supposed to cover for him, I guess.

DONNIE: *(Shaking his head and speaking slowly, as if he is just realizing something)* Maybe that explains . . .

CASSANDRA: What?

DONNIE: *(Excitedly)* Well, my dad and I were out jogging this morning around 5:15. We don't usually go out that early, but he and my mom are going away and . . .

CASSANDRA: *(Impatiently)* Get on with it, please! No one is interested with the details of your family's life.

DONNIE: *(Acting insulted)* Well, excuuuse me!

CASSANDRA: Well, come on!

DONNIE: Okay, okay. Well, I saw someone that looked like Jamar. I mean, I thought it was Jamar. But he was kinda far away. And when he looked at me, it was like he looked straight through me. It was like I wasn't even there. . . . He didn't wave or say hi or anything, you know? It was like he didn't know me. I just decided it wasn't Jamar after all. *(More slowly)* Or maybe he was hiding something. . . .

CASSANDRA: Then what happened? Is that it?

DONNIE: *(Now really interested in his own story)* Like I said, I thought that was really strange. But what was even more strange was that this guy was carrying bags of groceries with him. I couldn't figure it out. At 5:00 in the morning, most people are asleep. But if it was Jamar, he was coming from the all-night supermarket and heading in a direction away from home. (*He pauses, looks over at* CASSANDRA. *From her impatient look, he knows he had better get on with it.*) Yeah, there's more. We ran on past him and when we got down to the end of the block, I noticed that there were lights on at the old Weaver house. You know, the abandoned house. No one has lived there for at least a year. But I've been sort of watching the place and, well, there are some strange things going on there.

KELSIE: Like what?

CASSANDRA: (*Breaking in*) He's right! At night, when my mom is driving me home from karate class, we pass that house. There are lights on in there. And I've seen shadows of people moving around.

DONNIE: (*Picking up the cue*) Well, that must explain it.

KELSIE: (*Eagerly*) Explain what?

DONNIE: Well, on our way back, after Dad and I circled around the park, I saw that same guy, must have been Jamar, standing around the Weaver house like he was trying to make sure nobody saw him. Then he ducked along the side of the house and was gone.

KELSIE: (*Thinking intently*) Hmmmmm . . .

CASSANDRA: Hmmmm, what?

KELSIE: Well, I was just trying to put two and two together. . . .

CASSANDRA: You're thinking what I'm thinking.

DONNIE: Well, include me in on this.

CASSANDRA: We *are* supposed to be doing our Mystery Saturday project. . . .

DONNIE: . . . and Ms. Graves *didn't* say what kind of mystery it had to be. . . .

KELSIE: Just let me grab my coat.

(*Black out*)

SCENE 3: *Sunny hallway of the old Weaver house, with closed doorway at center stage. When this door is opened, audience should see a portion of the room behind it. The room will be bare except for a couple of chairs, a small lamp on the floor, a cassette player, and two double mattresses. The look is clean, not squalid.*

AT RISE: KELSIE, DONNIE, *and* CASSANDRA *are outside the door. From behind the door they hear music and the sound of* JAMAR'S *laughter. The three friends listen intently at the door, and then* KELSIE *impulsively opens it.* JAMAR *is sitting on the floor with instant photograph waste papers around him. He is looking happily at a stack of instant photos.*

JAMAR: Kelsie, where did you come from? Donnie! Cassandra! How's it going? Come here, I want to show you some friends. *(He points to a photograph.)* This is little Trey. He's only 2 years old. And this, this is Jason. He's 10 years old. My big man, Jason. See his eyes? He's blind. But he wasn't blind from birth. He had some kind of accident that, well . . . but the doctors say his sight will come back one day. And here, they're the parents, Mr. and Mrs. Wright. They've had some financial troubles since Jason's accident. What with all those operations and doctors' bills and all . . . They lost their house. *(His voice trails off.)* I've been sort of trying to help out while Mr. Wright was away. He was in Cleveland, looking for a job. We were just celebrating together because he found something real nice there. And they're moving on. They just left.

(JAMAR grows quiet. The other three stare at him.)

JAMAR: I would have told you, you know. But I had to keep it a secret. They could have gotten in trouble. Social services might have taken the kids away. Or the police might have arrested them for living here. You understand, don't you? *(He's talking to the room in general, but actually his comments are directed to KELSIE. She sits very still.)* Kelsie??

KELSIE: *(As if she's coming out of a daydream)* Jamar, I don't know what to say. Here I was thinking that you . . . I had no idea. . . . You were so preoccupied and strange and, well, what was I supposed to think?

The Strange Case of My Brother, or The Saturday Mystery ■ **107**

JAMAR: *(Soothingly)* Exactly what you thought.

KELSIE: *(Frantically)* No, but I should have. . . .

JAMAR: *(Gently)* . . . done exactly what you did.

(KELSIE *relaxes and runs to give* JAMAR *a hug. They laugh and punch each other playfully.*)

DONNIE: All right! *(Then becoming Sherlock Holmes again)* You see, my dear Cassandra, it was quite elementary. The parcels young Jamar carried with him this morning obviously held foodstuffs he purchased at the market with the money taken—or should we say "borrowed"?—from the family bank. The car that drove off as we arrived at the old Weaver place was not a getaway car but, rather, the Wright family vehicle heading easterly toward Cleveland. And, of course, the photographs. They all fit. I'd say another case is solved.

CASSANDRA: Precisely. *(Then sarcastically)* I just don't know how you do it!

KELSIE: *(Joining in on the fun and using a hint of a British accent herself)* Neither do I! *(Laughter all around)*

DONNIE: There is one other small matter that bothers me more than I care to think about.

KELSIE: And what is that?

DONNIE: *(In his own voice)* The Mystery Saturday Project.

JAMAR: *(Now he acts like Sherlock Holmes)* I think we may have already done it.

KELSIE: Elementary, my dear Donnie, elementary!

CASSANDRA: Let's get to the computer and write it up!

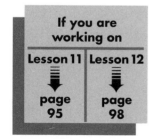

If you are working on

Lesson 11	Lesson 12
↓	↓
page 95	page 98

Elaine Epstein's poetry and essays have been published in national literary magazines. She attended the Writers' Workshop at the University of Iowa. Epstein grew up in New York, where both sets of her Russian grandparents immigrated. Today she lives in Houston, Texas.

The Heritage Project

by Elaine Epstein

As you read, take notes in the wide margins about story clues and what you already know to predict outcomes. You may also want to take notes about events that help lead to the solution of the problem presented in the play.

Characters

MR. DELAURA, *a high school social studies teacher*

LOUISA, *a 15-year-old student*

SETH, *another 15-year-old student*

ELISE GOLDBERG, *a 15-year-old classmate of Louisa and Seth*

YURI SOKOLOV, *a 15-year-old recent immigrant from the city of Odessa in the Russian Republics, a new classmate*

MR. GOLDBERG, *Elise's father*

PLAY COMPLETE IN ONE ACT.

SCENE 1

SETTING: MR. DELAURA's social studies classroom in a high school in suburban New York.

AT RISE: MR. DELAURA is in front of the class, leading a discussion.

MR. DELAURA: Now, where were we at the end of class yesterday?

LOUISA: We were talking about the different immigrant groups that came here in the . . . the . . . the . . .

SETH: . . . the 1880s or somewhere around then, right?

MR. DELAURA: Yes, that's right. We also discussed the pull factor and the push factor, if you recall. Some immigrant groups came because of difficult conditions in their homelands—the push. Other groups came for what they imagined were the great, golden opportunities in the United States—the pull. *(He notices ELISE, who is enthusiastically waving her hand to say something.)* Elise, do you have a question?

ELISE: In a book I read about a Chinese family in San Francisco's Chinatown, the United States was always called "Golden Mountain." Is that related to what you just said?

SETH: *(Leaning over to* ELISE, *whispering loudly in a snide tone)* Let me guess . . . you want an "A."

ELISE: *(Leaning over toward* SETH, *annoyed, whispering loudly back)* Yeah, I do. And I did read that. And I am interested in all of this, if you don't mind, Mr. Cynical.

SETH: *(Looking puzzled, still whispering)* What's "cynical" mean?

MR. DELAURA: "Cynical" means to question the sincerity of someone's feelings, motives, or actions, Seth. Does that answer your question? *(For a moment, the class erupts in laughter.)* And yes, Elise, golden mountain was the image many Chinese people had of the United States before they immigrated. But as you'll learn, the streets of United States cities were not always paved with gold for immigrants. Do you agree, Mr. Cynical? *(Said as a friendly tease to* SETH*)*

SETH: *(Sheepishly)* I really am interested in this subject. My great grandparents came to New York City from Poland.

MR. DELAURA: This subject—immigration to the United States—has personal significance for just about everyone. Because of that, I have a special project in mind. I want you to work in small groups. Each group will research one immigrant populace. We'll call this the Heritage Project, and I hope everyone learns something interesting about the heritage of his or her own family—or the family of a friend or neighbor. *(He divides the class into groups of four. One group consists of* ELISE, YURI, SETH, *and* LOUISA.*)*

ELISE: *(Talking privately to* LOUISA *as they walk to the corner where their small group will meet)* I can't believe Mr. DeLaura put Yuri in our group. He can't say much more than "Hello. How are you? Goodbye." *(Said in a monotone)* How will we put together a good presentation?

LOUISA: That's not fair, Elise. Yuri seems nice, even if he can't speak much English. And, he may be smarter than you think. Personally, I don't mind at all helping him.

ELISE: (*Looking over to YURI without his suspecting it, then turning to LOUISA*) Well, I'm not here to be an English teacher. I will admit, though, he has a nice smile.

LOUISA: You know, there may be a day when you need help from someone. Just remember that.
(*The group of four is now assembled.*)

YURI: Hello. How are you? I hope I can be assistance. Yes?

LOUISA: Better to say "of assistance," Yuri. (*She turns to ELISE and looks at her as if to say, "Be nice."*)

YURI: Thank you. I appreciate English of assistance.

LOUISA: You're welcome. But in that case you say only "assistance." It's confusing, but you'll catch on soon.

SETH: I have an idea. My family is from Poland. I think the rest of your families come from other countries in Eastern Europe. We're all Jewish—that is, Elise, Louisa, and myself are.

YURI: I, too, Jewishness.

LOUISA: You should say, "I am Jewish, too." (*Smiling at YURI*)

YURI: Thank you help, Louisa. (*He smiles back at LOUISA.*)

LOUISA: You're welcome. My pleasure.

ELISE: (*Anxious to move along with the group's task*) Okay. It's settled. We'll research the immigration of Jewish people from countries in Eastern Europe. And, because I think our group may need a little extra time (*She looks at LOUISA as if to say, "I told you so."*), how about if we meet at my house after school? (*In chorus everyone says "Sure." YURI chimes in a little late, looking to LOUISA to check his understanding of "Sure," an unfamiliar English expression.*)

SCENE 2

SETTING: *The living room of the Goldberg home*

AT RISE: ELISE, YURI, SETH, *and* LOUISA *are talking informally.* LOUISA *and* ELISE *are paired.*

LOUISA: You know, Elise, Yuri can make our project unique. He knows about immigration firsthand. We can interview him as part of our presentation.

YURI: *(Overhears* LOUISA *and comes over to her and* ELISE*)* What means "inner you," please?

ELISE: *(Trying to be patient)* Yuri, the word is "in-ter-view." An interview is when one person asks questions of another person, who gives answers. Can we interview you about your experience as a recent immigrant to the United States?

YURI: Yes, please. I, Yuri Sokolov. From Odessa, Russian Republic of Ukraine.

ELISE: Good idea, Louisa! *(Turns to face* YURI*)* Yuri, the interview will be good English practice for you. For now, though, tell us about Odessa.

YURI: *(Nods to show he understands)* Odessa beautiful place. On Black Sea. My family have business. Yes? But problem with Jewish. People . . . *(Struggling to find the English words he wants to use)* dislike Jewish. No reason.

ELISE and LOUISA: *(Interested)* Really?

YURI: *(Struggles for several moments, trying to find words; finally, he holds out his hand upon which he wears an antique gold ring.)* Family ring. Only thing Odessa left. *(He holds out his hand for* ELISE *and* LOUISA *to see the ring.)*

ELISE: It's beautiful. *(Turns toward other end of living room, where* SETH *is admiring an aquarium)* Seth, come here. Louisa has a great idea. We're going to interview Yuri for our presentation. We can introduce the interview with facts about Jewish immigrants from Eastern Europe in the late 1800s and early

1900s. We'll include photographs and stories from our own family histories.

(SETH, *having joined the group, nods in agreement.*)

YURI: *(Points to a tea set on the coffee table)* Samovar. *(He looks at* ELISE.) You, Russian, yes?

ELISE: Yes, but I don't know exactly from where. Wait a minute. *(She calls upstairs.)* Dad? Can you come down?

(MR. GOLDBERG *enters from his study upstairs, where he works as a science journalist.*)

ELISE: Dad, this is Yuri. He's from Odessa. He saw the tea set and asked if our family came from Russia. Where did your grandparents come from?

MR. GOLDBERG: *(Shaking hands with* YURI) Nice to meet you, Yuri. Well let's see. Elise's great

grandparents came here from Odessa. That's where the tea set—a samovar, as Russians call it—comes from. Israel Goldberg was my grandfather's name. Freida Sokolov (LOUISA *and* ELISE *gasp*) was my grandmother's name. They came to New York in 1900, with a short stopover on Ellis Island—just like every other immigrant did who entered the U.S. on the East Coast at that time.

LOUISA: *(Excited)* Mr. Goldberg, Yuri's last name is Sokolov! And he's from Odessa!

SETH: Maybe Sokolov is a common Russian—Jewish name—you know, like Smith or something?

ELISE: Yuri, show my father your family ring. Dad, Yuri said it's a ring from his family in Odessa.

MR. GOLDBERG: *(Scrutinizing the ring)* You know, that looks familiar somehow. Wait a minute.

(He leaves the room. Everyone sits quietly until he comes back. He is carrying a photograph album and a magnifying glass. He opens the album to pages of photographs of his grandparents and shows them to everyone. Then he hands the magnifying glass to ELISE.)

MR. GOLDBERG: This is your great grandmother Freida. Look at the picture closely.

ELISE: *(She studies the picture carefully with the magnifying glass.)* This is so weird! Yuri, my grandmother has a ring that looks something like yours!

LOUISA: *(Whispering to ELISE)* And you didn't think it would be worthwhile to work with Yuri on this project, Elise.

SETH: This will make a great addition to our presentation. And you'll get your "A," Elise!

YURI: Glad to be . . . of assistance. Right way to say—yes, umm, *(Says this word slowly and carefully)* cousin Elise?

ELISE: *(Leaning toward YURI)* You're catching on. *(Turning to MR. GOLDBERG)* Dad, can Yuri stay for dinner? After all he is family and we should make him feel at home.

Reviewing *Predicting Outcomes*

A. Read "The Heritage Project" on pages 109-114. As you read, use the wide margins to take notes about story clues and what you already know to help you make predictions. Then organize your ideas in the chart below.

Story Clues

Personal Experiences

+

Predictions or Outcomes

B. Imagine that you were assigned to a group project in which a group member spoke a language you did not speak. What could you do to work well with this student? Write your response in two or three sentences below.

Testing *Predicting Outcomes*

A. Each statement is a prediction of an outcome based on the play "The Heritage Project" on pages 109-114. Fill in the circle next to each prediction that makes sense. Then on the lines provided, explain why you did or did not fill in each circle.

○ By the end of Scene I, the reader might predict that Yuri and Elise will become good friends.

_____

_____

○ By the end of Scene I, the reader might predict that Louisa and Yuri might become good friends.

_____

_____

○ By the end of Scene I, the reader might predict that this group will have the most outstanding Heritage Project presentation.

_____

_____

○ When Elise calls her father downstairs in Scene 2, the reader might predict that Yuri and Elise will be friends because they have a lot in common.

_____

_____

B. Write a paragraph summarizing what might happen in a third scene for this play.

_____

_____

_____

_____

_____

_____

_____

_____

To begin Lesson 12 ⬇ page 98

Reviewing *Problem and Solution*

A. Read "The Heritage Project" on pages 109-114. As you read, use the wide margins to take notes on the problem, events that lead to its solution, and the turning point. Then organize your ideas in the chart below.

Title: _____

_____

Problem: _____

_____

Event 1: _____

_____

Event 2: _____

_____

Turning Point: _____

Solution: _____

B. Write about a project you have worked on with other classmates. In your passage, describe a problem and events that led to a solution. Make sure to identify the turning point.

_____

_____

_____

_____

_____

_____

_____

_____

_____

Testing **Problem and Solution**

A. Read the paragraphs below. Do not fill in any blanks. Then read the paragraphs again. As you read, select a word from the right column that makes sense in the sentence. Circle the word and write it on the line.

1. funny
   embarrassing
   sunny

2. uncomfortable
   older
   awful

3. clothes
   mother
   car

4. strobe lights
   flashlights
   candlelight

5. light
   dark
   bright

6. grandmother
   uncle
   mother

7. disastrous
   tiring
   good

8. Karen
   Juanita
   Joseph

9. mom
   uncle
   grandmother

"This is just great." Ana murmured. "The first chance I get to go out since we've moved here and my mother offers to be a chaperone! How _____!"
(1)

Reluctantly, Ana finally dragged herself downstairs, ready for an _____, not-so-fun evening. As they
(2)
approached South High, Ana saw some of her classmates standing outside the gym. She quickly hopped out of the car hoping they would not see her _____.
(3)

"Hey, Ana. You look great!" said Joseph. "Are you alone? Karen, Jaunita, and Jesse are inside. Let's go."

The gym seemed larger at night. Maybe it was the

_____, casting shadows on the walls in rhythm to
(4)
the beat of the music, thought Ana. In any case, it was so

_____ that Ana could barely see Joseph, with whom
(5)
she danced all night, let alone worry about her _____.
(6)

"Not such a _____ evening after all!" she
(7)
whispered to herself. She even contemplated introducing

_____ to her _____.
(8)   (9)

B. Imagine that you are Mr. DeLaura. What is a piece of advice you might give all the class groups to help them each develop good presentations for their heritage projects?

_____

_____

Unit SEVEN

BECOMING AN ACTIVE READER

Good readers are active readers. When reading **humorous essays,** they are ready for shocking twists of events or unexpected exaggerations—anything that writers use to persuade readers by making them laugh, or even cry.

Using Skills and Strategies

Identifying **humorous techniques** helps you understand the point that the writer is making in the essay. You might ask: What **techniques** has the writer used that make this essay funny? Why do they keep me interested in the subject? Are they effective in making the writer's point?

Using **context clues** to figure out the meaning of unfamiliar words will help you read actively. You might ask: What does this word mean? Which words in the same sentence or nearby sentences help me figure out the word's meaning?

In this unit, identifying **techniques of humor** and using **context clues** will help you as you read humorous essays.

Reading Humorous Essays

Reading essays gives us a chance to find out the writer's opinions, thoughts, and feelings on a subject. Most essays are serious but sometimes a writer will give us a lighter way to look at a subject or a chance to laugh at ourselves. You don't have to agree with the writer to enjoy reading the essay or to think the essay is effective. An essay is effective if you learn something new or see something in a new way.

Responding to the Essays

Good readers respond to an essay with an increased awareness of their own opinions about the subject. As you read the two essays in this unit, "Shark Treatment" and "Why Homemade Tortillas Are a Thing of the Past," make notes in the side margins about your own opinions. Use your notes when you discuss the essays with your classmates.

Reading Humorous Essays

| Lesson 13 | Introducing page 120 | Practicing page 121 | Applying page 122 | Reviewing page 132 | Testing page 133 |

Introducing Strategies

Sometimes writers use a humorous style to explain their feelings about a subject. In humorous essays, writers may use personification or exaggeration to make readers laugh and to keep them interested. Often, saying something unexpected, putting together two unlikely things, or telling an exaggerated story will get a humorous response. Good readers look for these and other **techniques of humor** as they read. They ask questions such as: Which humorous techniques is the writer using? How does the humor affect my response?

A chart like the one below shows how readers identify and respond to a writer's humorous style in an essay.

Question ▶	Think About ▶	Confirm
Which techniques of humor is the writer using?	What is the writer trying to say to the reader through this humorous style?	Is the humor engaging? Is it effective in conveying the message?

Reading Humorous Essays

Read the essay "Shark Treatment" and the sidenotes on pages 126-128. The notes show how one good reader identified and responded to the writer's use of humor. After reading, complete the items below.

1. List the examples of humor the reader identified.

_____

_____

_____

2. Explain how the reader knew the author was using humor.

_____

_____

_____

Practicing **Reading Humorous Essays**

A. The questions below are based on the essay "Shark Treatment." Circle the letter in front of the item that best answers each question. On the lines provided, identify the technique of humor.

1. Why do you think Dave Barry included the story about his experience with a shark?

    a. He wanted to make his essay longer.

    b. He thought it would make readers laugh.

    c. He wanted to show how people are in awe of sharks.

    d. I don't know. It really wasn't related to the topic of the essay.

_____

_____

2. What was Dave Barry's purpose in saying, "The primary food source of sharks today is bleeding fish pieces scattered by people making documentaries"?

    a. Sharks have a hard time finding food on their own.

    b. Too many shark documentaries are being made.

    c. It's important to feed the sharks.

    d. People who make documentaries are dedicated to preserving wildlife.

_____

_____

B. In your own words explain how Dave Barry feels about shark documentaries. Describe how humor helped convey his message. Be sure to include examples of humorous techniques used in the essay.

_____

_____

_____

_____

_____

_____

_____

_____

Applying *Reading Humorous Essays*

A. As you read the passage below, underline any examples of humor you identify. When you have finished reading, complete the items below.

> *To save energy, there should be no TV one day a week. That's what we need, one day a week when it would be illegal to watch TV. Tuesdays would be good. I have choir practice that night anyway (Aunt Minnie said it was important to get out of the house) and there are never any good TV shows on Tuesdays. People could pay attention to the drama in their own lives instead of that on TV. Quadrillions of kilowatt hours of electricity would not be used, saving billions of dollars in energy resources. And the TV set would have the vacation it deserves.*

1. Write two examples of humor you identified.

_____

_____

2. Describe how you identified them as humorous.

_____

_____

3. What is the writer's message in the passage? How did humor help convey that message?

_____

_____

B. Add a paragraph to the passage above. Use an exaggerated story to add humor.

_____

_____

_____

_____

_____

_____

_____

_____

To review
⬇
page
132

Context Clues

Introducing Strategies

Sometimes writers use words that are unfamiliar to readers. When good readers come across a word they don't know, they stop reading and look carefully at the meaning of words in the same sentence or in nearby sentences. These words provide **context clues** that can help readers figure out the meaning of the unfamiliar word.

Here's a checklist of questions readers can ask themselves as they look for context clues in their reading.

Question	YES	NO	If yes...
Are there context clues in the same sentence?	☐	☐	List the words, phrases.
Can I find a word or words in another sentence that mean about the same as the unfamiliar words?	☐	☐	Write the word or words.

Reading the Essay

Reread the essay "Shark Treatment" on pages 126-128. As you read, circle any unfamiliar words and underline the clues from the context that helped you figure out their meanings. Then complete the items below.

1. List three words you did not know. Write clues to their meanings from the context of the essay.

_____

_____

2. Write a definition for each word you chose.

_____

_____

_____

Practicing **Context Clues**

A. The sentences below are from the essay "Shark Treatment." Circle the letter next to the word or words that best defines the word in bold type. Then, on the lines provided, tell which context clues helped you make that choice.

1. "We **sprinted** I would say 600 yards in the opposite direction, using a sprinting style such that the bottoms of our feet never once went below the surface of the water."
   a. to leap
   b. to glide as if on skates
   c. to float
   d. to run very fast as for a short race

   _____

   _____

2. "Once the sharks arrive, they are generally fairly **listless**. The general shark attitude seems to be: 'Oh, God, another documentary.'"
   a. having no interest in what is happening
   b. exhausted
   c. excited
   d. angry

   _____

   _____

3. "One day, we were anchored near a little island that had a vast shallow sandy-bottomed **lagoon** next to it, maybe a foot deep . . ."
   a. a swimming pool
   b. a shallow pool of water that joins a large body of water
   c. a long bar or strip of sand
   d. an uninhabited, treeless island

   _____

   _____

B. Write a short summary on a topic you would like made into a television documentary. Use words readers might not be familiar with. Provide context clues to help define the words. Use another piece of paper to write your summary.

Applying *Context Clues*

A. Read the essay that follows. As you read, circle any words whose meaning you do not know. Then complete the items below.

> *I'm concerned about the quality of television advertisements. They've lost their positive appeal and have degenerated into frantic spectacles. They beg for viewers' attention with quick, loud flashes of words and actions. Critics complain about the violence in television programs. If my view is worth noting, I contend some advertisements are worse. They assault the senses: battering your eardrums, dizzying your eyes. Sure, I take a break when the commercials commence. As soon as an ad begins, I head for the kitchen. It's not to get a soda or snack that the advertisers are promoting, but to get away from the noise.*

1. List words in the essay that are unfamiliar to you.

_____

2. Write a definition for each word you listed. What clues from the context helped you figure out the meaning of each?

_____

_____

_____

B. Write a short essay about something you'd like to see changed. Use descriptive words. Be sure the context for each descriptive word is strong enough so that its meaning is clear.

_____

_____

_____

_____

_____

_____

_____

_____

_____

To review

↓

page 134

Dave Barry, a newspaper columnist for The *Miami Herald,* is a well-known humorist. His column appears regularly in several hundred newspapers nationwide. In 1988 he won the Pulitzer Prize, the highest honor a writer can receive. The essay below is from his book *Dave Barry's Greatest Hits.* It gives his ideas—presented with humor, of course—about creating a new TV show starring sharks.

Shark Treatment

by Dave Barry

The notes in the margin on page 126 show one reader's response to the essay. Notice how the notes show how the reader asked questions and confirmed the answers.

A TV program about people getting eaten by a shark? What's he talking about? Is he serious?

I have come up with a sure-fire concept for a hit television show, which would be called "A Live Celebrity Gets Eaten by a Shark." To help you understand why I think this show would be a success, let me give you a little background.

I'm curious about the beauty in nature, too. I wonder about things that seem impossible. I'm also sometimes curious about the violence.

The human race has been fascinated by sharks for as long as I can remember. Just like the bluebird feeding its young, or the spider struggling to weave its perfect web, or the buttercup blooming in spring, the shark reveals to us yet another of the infinite and wonderful facets of nature, namely the facet that can bite your head off. This causes us humans to feel a certain degree of awe.

I know what I'm talking about here, because I once had—this is the truth—an encounter with a shark. It was in 1973, in the Bahamas, where I was sailing with a group of friends. One day, we were anchored near a little island that had a vast shallow sandy-bottomed lagoon next to it, maybe a foot deep, and a friend of mine named Richard and I were wading around in there, and lo and behold we saw this shark. It was a small shark, less than two feet long. The only conceivable way it could have been a threat to a human being would be if it somehow got hold of, and learned to use, a gun.

What? Now he's talking about a sailing trip. A shark using a gun? Now I know he wants me to smile.

So Richard and I decided to try to catch it. With a great deal of strategy and effort and shouting, we managed to maneuver the shark, over the course of about a half-hour, to a sort of corner of the lagoon, so that it had no way to escape other than to flop up onto the land and evolve. Richard and I were inching toward it, sort of crouched over, when all of a sudden it turned around and—I can still remember the sensation I felt at that moment, primarily in the armpit area—*headed right straight toward us.*

What does he mean escape by flopping "onto the land and evolve"? Sharks can't evolve into something else that quickly. He's exaggerating. He's trying to be funny.

Many people would have panicked at this point. But

Write your own sidenotes as you finish reading the essay. Focus on how the author used humor to explain how he feels about the subject.

Richard and I were not "many people." We were experienced waders, and we kept our heads. We did exactly what the textbook says you should do when you're unarmed and a shark that is nearly two feet long turns on you in water up to your lower calves: We sprinted I would say 600 yards in the opposite direction, using a sprinting style such that the bottoms of our feet never once went below the surface of the water. We ran all the way to the far shore, and if we had been in a Warner Brothers cartoon you would have seen these two mounds of sand racing across the island until they bonked into trees and coconuts fell onto their heads.

So I know the fascination of the shark, and thus I have been particularly interested in all these shark documentaries on television. You've probably noticed them. Any given night, you tune into a channel at random and odds are you'll see divers hurling themselves into shark-infested waters. The narrator always claims this is for Scientific Research, which is blatant horse waste. I mean, if that were true, you'd figure that after two or three thousand documentaries, they'd know all they needed to know about sharks, and they'd move on to another variety of sea life. But they don't, because they know darned good and well that the viewers aren't going to remain glued to their seats to watch divers paddling around in waters infested by, for example, clams.

So the documentary-makers stick with sharks. Generally, their procedure is to scatter bleeding fish pieces around their boat, so as to infest the waters. I would estimate that the primary food source of sharks today is bleeding fish pieces scattered by people making documentaries. Once the sharks arrive, they are generally fairly listless. The general shark attitude seems to be: "Oh, God, another documentary." So the divers have to somehow goad them into attacking, under the guise of Scientific Research. "We know very little about the effect of electricity on sharks," the narrator will say, in a deeply scientific voice. "That is why Todd is going to jab this Great White. . . with a cattle prod." The divers keep this kind of thing up until the shark finally gets irritated and snaps at them, and then they act as though this was a totally unexpected and very dangerous development, although clearly it is what they wanted all along.

Shark documentaries took an important stride forward recently with a series called "Ocean Quest," in which, instead of using trained divers, the documentary maker rented a former beauty queen, Shawn Weatherly,

Shark Treatment ■ **127**

and spent a year dropping her into various shark-infested waters. The idea was that she, being a regular person just like me and you except she has a great body, would be able to convey to us viewers the various human emotions she was feeling. This was pretty funny, inasmuch as Shawn's acting ability is such that she could not convey the concept of falling if you pushed her off a cliff. But the point is, here was a shark documentary that barely even pretended to be scientific, and instead focused on the excitement involved in watching somebody act as bait.

So I say it's time to take this one step farther. I say the public is ready to drop the Scientific Research aspect altogether. . . . I don't think it would be a problem, getting the celebrities. You look for somebody whose career really needs a boost—a Telly Savalas, for example, or a Zsa Zsa Gabor—and you point out what exposure like this could do for a person. I don't think you could keep Zsa Zsa *out* of the water. Ed McMahon could be the host. Your only real problem would be getting a shark. Most of your top sharks probably have commitments to do documentaries.

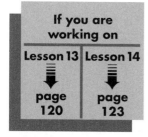

If you are working on

Lesson 13	Lesson 14
⬇	⬇
page 120	page 123

Frank Sifuentes, who owns a successful communications business and is very active in the Los Angeles Latino community, has watched the tortilla business grow in southern California for four decades. He sponsors tortilla-making contests, and uses the proceeds for scholarships for Latino high schoolers. In this essay, Sifuentes writes about the art of tortilla making.

Why Homemade Tortillas Are a Thing of the Past

by Frank Moreno Sifuentes

As you read, use the margin to note how the author used humor to describe his thoughts about the subject and what you think he is really trying to say.

My mother-in-law, Chavelita Diaz, was one of the great masters of the art of making flour tortillas. She was the oldest daughter of a family from Mexico who immigrated to Los Angeles in the early part of the century. As the oldest daughter, she inherited the role of "tortilla maker" in her family. In those days, the role was a desirable one. A good tortilla maker was praised and admired.

Chavelita's grill, called a *comal,* had originally been part of an old pot-belly stove. It was small and she used it in Mexico to make perfect *tortillas de maiz* (tortillas made from corn meal). But Chavelita, like most Mexican women who came to live in the United States, discovered that white flour made from refined wheat was more readily available here and less expensive than corn meal. So, she started making flour tortillas on her *comal.*

Chavelita began using a recipe for white flour tortillas that had been handed down through generations. It had been brought to Mexico by the Spaniards in the 1500s. The recipe for flour tortillas was used in Mexico on special occasions. The ingredients are white refined flour, lard, baking powder, and salt. The exact combination remains a secret. Anyway, the tortillas were by far the most delicious and perfectly made I have ever tasted. They were better than any made on my side of the family—better than Mamagrande Lupe's or Tia Lupe's. Quite simply, Chavelita's were the best.

I loved watching Chavelita's tortillas rise. It happened so fast that each tortilla looked like a little balloon. Sometimes I thought they'd float to the ceiling! Chavelita would calmly press down on them with her rolling pin, giving each one a single turn. This was part of her technique. When those tortillas came off the grill, they were quickly buttered. Eating them hot was like going to heaven.

You can see how I felt about Chavelita's tortilla making. It was like perfection! I admired and appreciated it so much. My wife, Sara, and our children felt the same. Chavelita's art was encouraged by economic necessity, but motivated by love.

Can you understand, then, why I felt a bit baffled when Sara decided that the *comal* duties were not for her? In fact, she did everything she could to avoid making tortillas.

My children and I soon found ourselves eating store-bought white bread. Complaining did not help. We were told that we had better learn to like it.

How did this happen? How did tortilla-making go from a respected art to a distasteful chore? Remember, by the late 1950s, most Latinas were out earning "the bread," just like their husbands. After a long day at work, they had little time or energy to break out the ingredients for tortillas, mix them, heat the *comal*, and laboriously roll and cook dozens of tortillas. They especially hated the way family members would sit there, impatiently waiting for the next tortilla to come off the grill.

Being thick-headed about these ideas, I only increased the pressure on my wife. I formed an alliance with our children. Together we would whine, plead, and beg for Sara to make tortillas.

About half the time we would win. My wife would slam things around in the kitchen, muttering about how spoiled we were. But she would make the tortillas. Women's liberation remained only half won.

Fortunately for my wife, the giant of capitalism never sleeps. The tortilla-making machine was invented! My wife, like other Latinas, raced to the supermarket to buy the factory-made tortillas.

The taste, texture, and appearance of these first factory-made tortillas were disappointing. My son Andrew, a chip off the old block, called them "fake tortillas." Nevertheless, store-bought tortillas became our mainstay. As my wife said, "If you don't like them, eat bread instead."

By the late 1960s, these tortillas had improved. With this improvement came increased resolution among Latinas never to make tortillas at home.

By the late 1970s, the debate was dead. Store-bought tortillas had replaced home-made tortillas.

By the mid-1980s, I was feeling a wave of tortilla nostalgia that wouldn't go away. I decided that if Latinas would no longer make tortillas at home, it was the men's turn. And so I began a tortilla revolution!

I began making flour tortillas using what I called the "for-men-only secret recipe." My tortillas were tasty, but they weren't round. Instead, they resembled the different shapes of states. The problem was, I never knew which state might pop up!

Then I started a charity event, a tortilla-making contest "for men only." The contest was exciting to watch, since it was hands-on. Lots of men entered. There they stood, laboring over their rolling pins and hot *comals*, as the women watched, snickering and smirking. I asked large tortilla-making companies to support our event. They, however, declined the opportunity. They were afraid that if tortilla-making by men became a fad, their business would not continue its phenomenal growth.

These business owners do not realize one important fact. Any man who makes home-made tortillas a few times reaches the same conclusion: Store-bought tortillas are, after all, very good! Still, I can't help wishing for just one more of Chavelita's flour tortillas.

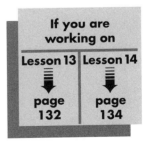

If you are working on

Lesson 13	Lesson 14
↓	↓
page 132	page 134

Reviewing **Reading Humorous Essays**

A. Read the essay "Why Homemade Tortillas Are a Thing of the Past" on pages 129-131. As you read, look for examples of the author's use of humor. When you have finished, complete the chart below.

Question ▶	**Think About** ▶	**Confirm**
Which techniques of humor is the writer using?	What is the writer trying to say to the reader through this humorous style?	Is the humor engaging? Is it effective in conveying the message?

B. Identify a food you particularly like or dislike. How strong are your feelings about it? Describe the food as humorously—as outrageously as you can. Be sure to use humorous comparisons and exaggerations.

_____

_____

_____

_____

_____

_____

_____

_____

_____

_____

Testing **Reading Humorous Essays**

A. The sentences below are from "Why Homemade Tortillas Are a Thing of the Past" on pages 129-131. Read each pair of sentences. Put an X next to the sentence in which the author has used humor to make a point. On the lines, describe the humorous technique.

1. ___ It happened so fast that each tortilla looked like a little balloon.

___ Sometimes I thought they'd float to the ceiling!

_____

2. ___ Being thick-headed about these ideas, I only increased the pressure on my wife.

___ I formed an alliance with our children.

_____

3. ___ My son Andrew called them "fake tortillas."

___ Nevertheless, store-bought tortillas became our mainstay.

_____

4. ___ I began making flour tortillas using what I called the "for-men-only secret recipe."

___ The problem was, I never knew which state might pop up!

_____

B. Write an essay about something store-bought that you like better homemade. Describe how the two are different. Explain why you think it should be made by hand more often.

_____
_____
_____
_____
_____
_____
_____

To begin
Lesson 14

page
123

Reviewing **Context Clues**

A. Reread "Why Homemade Tortillas Are a Thing of the Past" on pages 129-131. Underline words that you are unfamiliar with or whose meaning you do not know. When you have finished, complete the checklist below showing how you used context clues to figure out the meaning of some of the unfamiliar words.

Question	YES	NO	If yes...
Are there context clues in the same sentence? _____ _____	☐	☐	List the words, phrases. _____ _____
Can I find a word or words in another sentence that mean about the same as the unfamiliar words? _____ _____	☐	☐	Write the word or words. _____ _____ _____

B. Describe a tradition or custom that is important in your family. Circle any special words you use that a reader might not be familiar with. Include clues in your paragraph that would help the reader figure out the meanings.

_____

_____

_____

_____

_____

_____

_____

_____

Testing **Context Clues**

A. The words below are from the essay "Why Homemade Tortillas Are a Thing of the Past." Read the essay through once. Then read it again. Fill in each blank with a word from the list that makes the best sense. Underline the context clues.

I wanted to go to college and become a chef. But how would I pay for it? Then I had an idea. Why not apply for one of the best _____ my high school awards at graduation? Well, my first problem was that I would have to write an essay about why I deserved to get the money! What would I say? How would I say it? Could I sound convincing? At first, the problem _____ me. I had to stop worrying and get to work. My dream for a good education _____ me to try my hardest. This was not just a good opportunity—to me it was _____! Of course, I knew I wasn't the only person applying, so I felt a lot of _____. I had to write the essay now—RIGHT NOW—and to write it well—REALLY WELL! I worked for days. I outlined ideas, put sentences on paper, crumpled paper, crumpled more paper, and started over. And over. I was determined to do a good job. At last I liked what I had written. Can you guess what happened? My _____ to do a good job paid off. I won!

baffled

pressure

motivated

resolution

phenomenal

scholarships

B. Write a humorous essay about scholarships. Should a student be required to write a personal essay? Or should the student's record in school be enough? Write notes for your essay here.

_____

_____

Unit EIGHT

BECOMING AN ACTIVE READER

Good readers are critical readers. When they read **persuasive essays** they decide for themselves if they agree with the writer's viewpoint. Good readers bring an open mind to new ideas. They also use their own thoughts and experiences to evaluate a writer's position.

Using Skills and Strategies

Learning to recognize **cause and effect** relationships will help you read persuasive essays critically. You might ask: What happened as a result of this event? What caused this particular situation? How do the causes or effects stated in the essay help support the writer's position?

Identifying the **main ideas** and using them to **summarize** what you've read is a way to organize the writer's thoughts presented in an essay. Ask yourself: What are the most important ideas in this passage? Which ideas support the writer's viewpoint?

In this unit, the skills of identifying **cause and effect** relationships and using **main ideas** to **summarize** will help you read the essays critically.

The Persuasive Essay: The Writer's Voice

Writing persuasive essays is an effective way for people from diverse backgrounds to inform readers about the ideas, viewpoints, and needs that grow out of their particular cultural experiences. Essays that promote new ways of looking at issues can broaden a reader's perspective and can lead to greater understanding and tolerance.

Responding to Stories

Good readers respond to persuasive essays by comparing their own feelings and attitudes about the subject with those of the writer. It is helpful to jot down your reactions as you read the essays "Why—and How—the BIA Should Be Dissolved" and "Why Asians Should Play Asian Roles." Use the margins for your notes. Use these notes when you discuss the essays with your classmates.

Cause and Effect

| Lesson 15 | Introducing page 137 | Practicing page 138 | Applying page 139 | Reviewing page 149 | Testing page 150 |

Introducing Strategies

In persuasive essays, writers want readers to think in a certain way. To do this, they often present **cause and effect** relationships to support their opinions. Causes are the reasons something happens. The effects are the results. The next time you read a persuasive essay or article, notice the cause and effect relationships that the writer uses. Ask yourself: Does this relationship clarify the writer's position? Does it influence my thinking?

The chart below shares how readers can keep track of cause and effect relationships while reading persuasive essays.

| CAUSE (the reason) | ⟹ | EFFECT (the result) |

Reading the Persuasive Essay

Read the essay "Why—and How—the BIA Should Be Dissolved" on pages 143-145 and the sidenotes on pages 143-144. The sidenotes show how one good reader identified cause and effect relationships.

1. How does the reader say Native Americans view the BIA? Why?

_____

_____

_____

2. What does the reader note has happened as a result of the BIA's intervention in the lives of Native Americans?

_____

_____

_____

_____

Practicing *Cause and Effect*

A. Each incomplete statement below is based on the essay about the BIA on pages 143-145. Circle the letter next to the phrase that best completes each cause and effect relationship. Then explain your choice.

1. According to the writer, if the BIA becomes an equal partner to Native Americans, it will
   a. create chaos.
   b. gradually phase itself out of existence.
   c. help Native Americans find jobs off the reservations.
   d. make Native Americans more dependent.

   _____

   _____

2. One reason that Native Americans are concerned about the government's use of their land and resources is that
   a. Native Americans don't belive in land ownership.
   b. the BIA is in the Department of the Interior.
   c. the BIA follows *Robert's Rules of Order.*
   d. Native Americans enjoy fishing.

   _____

   _____

3. The Pit River Nation feels that it is able to govern itself, so it has chosen to
   a. remain independent of the BIA.
   b. receive full federal benefits.
   c. waste time talking with the BIA.
   d. accept the policies of the BIA.

   _____

   _____

B. Identify two cause and effects the author has stated that are particularly effective in supporting his position. Explain why.

   _____

   _____

   _____

   _____

   _____

Applying *Cause and Effect*

A. Read the passage below. Then answer the questions that follow.

HOW TO PREPARE FOR YOUR JOB INTERVIEW

Sam showed up for his job interview at a fast-food chain with uncombed hair and dirty fingernails. Bob interviewed for the same job looking neat and clean. Bob got the job. Sam is still looking for work.

Before her job interview, Mary went to the library and did some research on the company she hoped to work for on weekends. Betsy thought that was too much trouble for a part-time job. The interviewer was impressed by Mary's efforts and hired her. Betsy is still looking for work.

What is the lesson to be learned from these case studies? Before interviewing for a job, do your homework. Then make sure your first impression is a good one.

1. According to the essay, what caused Bob and Mary to get their jobs?

_____

_____

2. Why weren't Sam and Betsy hired?

_____

_____

3. What effects do you think the writer hopes his advice will have?

_____

_____

B. Write a brief persuasive essay on some topic related to work. In your essay, use at least two cause and effect relationships to help make your point.

_____

_____

_____

_____

_____

To review

↓

page 149

Summarizing

Introducing Strategies

Summarizing helps readers organize important information and clarify what they have read. Good readers summarize what they read by looking for the writer's topic, or central idea. Then they identify main ideas that support the topic and restate them briefly in their own words.

Using a chart like the one below helps readers summarize what they have read based on the writer's main ideas.

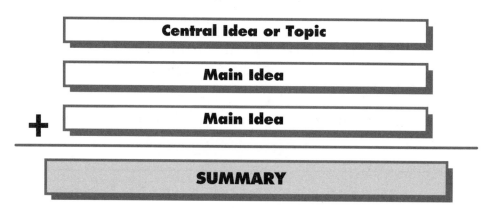

Reading the Persuasive Essay

Reread the essay "Why—and How—the BIA Should Be Dissolved" on pages 143-145. As you read, underline the main ideas in the essay and identify the topic, or author's central message.

1. What is the topic of this essay?

_____

_____

_____

_____

2. List two main ideas that reflect the ideas the author is making.

_____

_____

_____

Practicing Summarizing

A. Each pair of sentences below is based on the essay "Why—and How—the BIA Should Be Dissolved" on pages 143-145. Place a check in front of the sentence that states a main idea and could be used in a summary of the essay. Then explain your choices on the lines provided.

1. ___The BIA has had a negative impact on the lives of most Native Americans.

   ___The BIA has 12 regional centers in the United States.

   _____

   _____

2. ___The BIA originally was part of the Department of War.

   ___Because the BIA is set up to direct, not be a partner to, Native Americans, numerous frustrations arise.

   _____

   _____

3. ___The BIA is unnecessary because only Congress can make or regulate laws regarding Native Americans.

   ___The writer comes from the Pit River Nation.

   _____

   _____

4. ___The writer grew up in California.

   ___The writer believes that the BIA can be dissolved naturally.

   _____

   _____

B. Write a short paragraph that summarizes your own reaction to the ideas in the essay "Why—and How—the BIA Should Be Dissolved."

_____

_____

_____

_____

_____

Applying *Summarizing*

Read the passage below. After you read it, answer the questions that follow.

STOP "JUNK" TELEPHONE CALLS

Telephone solicitations are at best nuisances and at worst scams. Yet many people put up with invasions of their privacy from high-tech salesmen who interrupt mealtimes, wake up babies, and generally become unwelcome intruders into private homes.

What can you do? Some people suggest passing a law to make it illegal for solicitors to call people who designate in the phone book that they do not want to be solicited. Another suggestion is to tax telemarketing companies and use revenues to reduce costs of basic phone service to customers. But until lawmakers do something, individual homeowners can take action! For instance, plan how you will respond to phone solicitors—"Thank you, I'm not interested" followed by hanging up. "I'm busy, but give me your home number and I'll call back." Post your ideas near your phone. When you answer a "junk" phone call, be firm. Remember—it's your privacy being invaded!

1. What is the central message of the passage?

_____

_____

_____

2. List the main points in each paragraph.

_____

_____

_____

_____

3. Write a brief summary of the passage in the space below.

To review
↓
page
151

_____

_____

_____

_____

Darryl Babe Wilson grew up in the extreme northeastern corner of California. His people, the Pit River Nation, are called an unrecognized nation because they have remained independent of the Bureau of Indian Affairs (BIA). In this article, Wilson shares his views regarding the BIA and its usefulness.

Why—and How—the BIA Should Be Dissolved

by Darryl Babe Wilson

The notes in the margins on pages 143-144 show how one reader identified causes and effects.

The Bureau of Indian Affairs (BIA) had its beginnings in 1806. It was established as the Office of Superintendent of Indian Trade and was part of the Department of War. In 1849, it was renamed and moved to the Department of the Interior. Today the BIA has 12 regional centers around the United States.

Throughout its long history, the BIA has been the least powerful of all government agencies. Typically, it is viewed as nothing more than a social welfare system that gives away too much money and food to Native Americans. In fact, the BIA administers government programs that provide welfare services and education to Native Americans living on reservations. The BIA also establishes land-use programs on reservations and helps find jobs off reservations. The result of such a set-up has been negative for most Native Americans. We fear that the BIA gives the impression that we are helpless, dependent people.

◀ Native Americans seem to view the BIA as an ineffective government program. What has caused this?

◀ Here, the writer says that the reason is that the BIA's program treats Native Americans as if they are helpless.

Yet whenever there is talk of dismantling the BIA, there is loud argument among Native Americans. Some want the agency to be dissolved at once. They say that it represents the historical injustice of the U.S. government toward Native Americans. Past unfair treatment by government agencies makes many Native Americans distrust the motives of current agencies, especially when disagreements occur. Others fear the ending of the agency. They say that all trust between Native Americans and the U.S. government would also end.

◀ In this paragraph, the writer shows that as a result, a controversy has developed among Native American groups. Some want it dissolved; others fear that if it's dissolved they'll destroy relations with the United States government.

I believe that the BIA can be dissolved naturally, without the need for big debates and hard decisions. If the agency becomes what it should be—an equal partner to Native Americans, not a director—it will quietly phase itself out of existence.

Reasons the BIA Is Unsatisfactory

To those who would argue that the BIA already functions as a partner, I present the following frustrations. All of these come from the fact that the BIA is set up to be our director, not our equal.

I had to reread this paragraph! Although frustrations are mentioned first, they are really effects; the way the BIA is set up is the cause for the frustrations.

Write your own notes in the margins identifying cause and effect relationships.

Conflicting Styles

The BIA is highly inaccessible to the people it is supposed to help. If we do get a chance to be heard by the BIA, we are not allowed to express ourselves in a way we find familiar and comfortable. Our way is to sit together, council-style. Together, we reach an agreement. The BIA way is to follow *Roberts' Rules of Order*. The meeting follows a chain of command, from the top down. We, of course, are on the bottom.

Conflicting Interests

The BIA is part of the Department of the Interior, which has authority over land, minerals, water, and other resources. Native Americans are especially concerned about the sacredness of these things. Reservations are practically the only spots left in the United States (besides state and federal parks) where land and minerals have been used wisely and preserved. Since our reservations are now under the Department of Interior's authority, the government is able to use our lands and resources to meet the needs of the majority.

In Washington, for example, the Department of Fish and Game has been at odds with Native Americans for years over fishing rights. At one time, an agreement was made regarding one river in the state. People fishing in the river were to pay attention to an "imaginary line" running down the middle of this river. Native Americans could fish on one side, and commercial companies could fish on the other side. Once, a Native American was accused by a game warden of fishing beyond the imaginary line. The fisherman's response, "I thought the imaginary line was over there," reveals some of the frustration with the rule. Native Americans find it hard to figure out rules that try to make nature "belong" to anyone. We do not understand how anyone can own the land we walk on any more than anyone could own the air we breathe.

Who Governs Native American Nations?

As Supreme Court Justice Ruth Ginsburg pointed out in 1993, any matter pertaining to Native American nations should *by law* be settled by Congress. According to the Constitution, the U.S. Congress is the only governing body that can make or regulate laws regarding our people. If this is so, the BIA is unnecessary.

However, contrary to the law, the Department of the Interior has organized our people into four groups, according to our willingness to work with the government:

- Federally Recognized: These groups receive federal benefits and assistance and are "on record" as a political group (like "Puerto Ricans" or "Vietnamese Americans").

- State Recognized: These groups receive state benefits and are "on record" as a political group.

- Terminated: These groups have formally cut off any ties with the federal government.

- Unrecognized: These groups do not receive state or federal benefits. They have not organized themselves in the way the Department of the Interior requires.

I come from the Pit River Nation, which is unrecognized. We feel that we are traditionally sovereign. This means that we govern ourselves in our traditional ways, through agreements among ourselves. We do not choose to waste our time with organizations like the BIA. In our way of thinking, only Congress has any legal power over us.

A Lack of Respect for our Ways

BIA officials suggest laws regarding the governing of our people to the Secretary of the Interior. Yet, these laws are suggested without consulting our people. The attitude is that the government knows the needs of the Native Americans. Laws are made, and Native Americans are pressured to accept them. Few, if any, Native Americans believe that this works well.

Change and Compromise

I don't think we have to eliminate the BIA. I think it can be phased out. Compromise between the BIA and Native American nations can result in a partnership that will help us attain our rightful legal standing in Congress. For this, we must wait patiently, drawing on the strength of our customs and traditions.

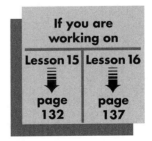

If you are
working on

Lesson 15	Lesson 16
⬇	⬇
page 132	page 137

Angela Chen is an Asian American journalist who has been exposed to many different cultures. She grew up in Panama and speaks English, Spanish, and the Chinese dialect Hakka. Although Chen focuses on Asian cultures, she stresses that her comments in this persuasive essay should apply to all cultural groups.

Why Asians Should Play Asian Roles

by Angela Chen

One of the big issues today in the world of plays and movies involves the casting of ethnic roles. The issue was brought to a head in 1990 with the controversy surrounding the play *Miss Saigon*. When this play was produced in London, Jonathan Pryce played the lead role. Pryce is a European actor, and his character was Eurasian (European Asian). Many people in the theater world and beyond disapproved of this casting. Why, they wondered, wouldn't an Asian be cast in the role?

When *Miss Saigon* was brought to New York City, Actor's Equity (an organization of 40,000 U.S. performers) protested the casting of Pryce. Fifteen other community groups supported Actor's Equity. The controversy became very heated. At one point, the producer of the play said he would cancel the show in New York if Pryce were not allowed to play the role. This would have cost more than 40 Asian Americans who *did* have roles in the play their jobs. Eventually, Actor's Equity gave in. Pryce was allowed to play the role on Broadway.

The controversy surrounding the decision has not gone away, however. The facts remain the same. Asian actors bring a rich cultural background to Asian roles. They are able to understand the roles more fully than non-Asians are. They are more sensitive to Asian issues. For these reasons, they are better prepared than non-Asians to play the roles. Yet discrimination in the United States entertainment industry still results in the casting of non-Asians in starring roles.

The Changes in U.S. Culture

The ethnic make-up of the United States has changed in the past 20 years. As part of this change, the number of

Asian Americans has more than doubled. By the year 2000, about 5 percent of the total U.S. population, or 10 million people, will be Asian American. Asian Americans represent many different cultural groups, including Chinese, Vietnamese, Japanese, Korean, Cambodian, Filipino, Thai, and Hmong, among others. They have fanned out from their first points of entry to just about every region in the United States. This means that throughout the United States, greater numbers of Asian Americans will be seeking job opportunities in all areas, including acting.

The Practice of Nontraditional Casting

It is common in the entertainment business for actors to play roles whether or not they match the characters in race, ethnicity, and even gender. Although the job of an actor is to pretend to be someone different from whom he or she is, Asian Americans should play Asian American roles when a character's ethnicity is critical to the context of the movie or play.

Problems with Nontraditional Casting

In *Miss Saigon*, the producer, Cameron Mackintosh, cast whites in leading Asian roles. He was following tradition when he did so. Throughout the history of the entertainment industry, directors have used white actors and actresses—including Marlon Brando as Sakini in *The Teahouse of the August Moon*, Angie Dickinson in *China Gate*, Yul Brynner as the king in *The King and I*, and John Gielgud as Chang in *Lost Horizon*—to play Asian roles. The result of such casting decisions is often a performance that is less than convincing. A more serious result is the continuance of stereotypes. For example, heavy make-up is often used to make actors "look" Asian. Actors and actresses often take on the mannerisms of stereotypical Asians. For example, women might act meekly, bow, and take tiny steps. Such inaccuracy in looks and characterization helps perpetuate racial stereotypes.

Sometimes the industry's tendency to place whites at the center of events has even resulted in distortions of history. For example, the movie *Mississippi Burning* presented brave white F.B.I. agents coming to the rescue of African Americans—the reverse of what actually happened. The director of the film, Alan Parker, answered his critics in this way: "Because it is a movie, I felt it had to be fictionalized. The two heroes in the story had to be white. That is a reflection of our society as much as of the film industry."

When ethnicity is involved, producers should at least consult with the ethnic group for accuracy. In producing and directing *Dances with Wolves*, a movie about Native Americans, Kevin Costner consulted often with Native American authorities. He also cast Rodney Grant, a Native American actor, in a lead role. This extra work enhanced the success of the movie—it was named best picture of 1990!

Struggling for Parts

Asian Americans often are called the "model minority," the people whose hard work has helped them to achieve the "American dream." In reality, however, a majority of Asian Americans are struggling for equal status and recognition. This is especially true in the theater.

The casting director for *Miss Saigon*, Vincent G. Liff of the Johnson, Liff & Zerman casting agency, said that he was not able to find an Asian actor "suitable" for the role—one of more or less the right age who could act and sing. Mackintosh, the producer of the play, said a search was done worldwide for actors of Asian heritage to play the many different Asian roles. The search was indeed much publicized. However, it actually centered on casting the starring role of Kim, the young Asian woman. No actor but Jonathan Pryce was seriously considered for the leading male role. Therefore, there was not the sort of "good faith effort" Asians had expected.

In a perfect world, any artist should be able to play any role for which he or she is suited. Until that time arrives, however, artists of color must fight for the few roles that are culturally specific to them. In the diverse United States of today, equal opportunity in any area must not be denied. Besides, plays and movies can be made richer by the cultural background brought by Asians in leading roles.

If you are
working on

Lesson 15	Lesson 16
⬇	⬇
page 149	page 151

Reviewing *Cause and Effect*

A. Read the essay "Why Asians Should Play Asian Roles" on pages 146-148. As you read, make notes in the margin when you identify a cause and effect relationship. Then use your sidenotes to complete the chart below.

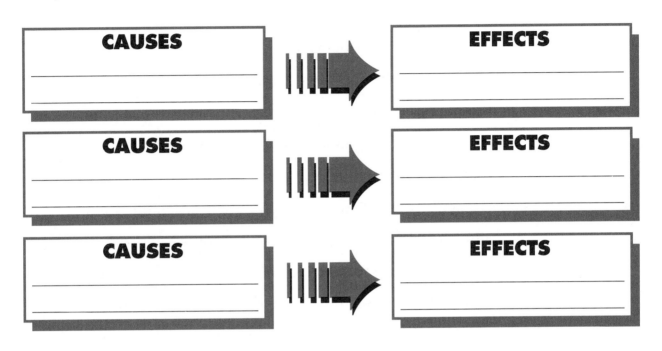

CAUSES → **EFFECTS**

CAUSES → **EFFECTS**

CAUSES → **EFFECTS**

B. On the lines below, explain the effects caused by casting white performers in nonwhite roles.

_____

_____

_____

_____

_____

_____

_____

_____

_____

_____

_____

_____

Testing *Cause and Effect*

A. The paragraph below is based on the essay "Why Asians Should Play Asian Roles" on pages 146-148. Fill in each blank with a word that you think makes the most sense in the sentence.

Because a European actor was cast in the role of a Eurasian in the play *Miss Saigon,* Actor's Equity and community groups _____. "Why not cast an _____ actor in an Asian American role when the character's ethnicity is critical to the plot line?" people protested. Actor's Equity finally gave in when the producer threatened to _____ the show's New York run if Pryce, the European actor scheduled for the lead, was not allowed to play the role. If the show were canceled, more than 40 Asian American actors who were to work in the show would have _____ their jobs. However, many people still believe that Asian actors playing Asian roles are better able to understand the characters they play than _____ actors, because of their cultural _____ and heritage.

B. Write a paragraph that describes the effects that you think casting Asian Americans in Asian roles might have in movies and the theater.

_____

_____

_____

_____

_____

_____

_____

_____

To begin
Lesson 16

↓

page
140

Reviewing *Summarizing*

A. Reread the essay "Why Asians Should Play Asian Roles" on pages 146-148. Circle main ideas as you read. Then complete the chart below, filling in the main ideas you have identified and then summarizing them in the bottom box.

Topic _____

Main Idea _____
_____

Main Idea _____
_____

+

SUMMARY _____
_____
_____

B. Choose a topic for a persuasive essay you might like to write. Think about the main ideas you would include, then write a summary of what your essay might say.

_____
_____
_____
_____
_____
_____
_____
_____

Testing Summarizing

A. Fill in the circle next to each statement that summarizes the main ideas in the essay "Why Asians Should Play Asian Roles" on pages 146-148. Then, on the lines provided, explain why you did or did not fill in the oval.

○ Marlon Brando played the role of Sakini in *The Teahouse of the August Moon.*

_____

_____

○ Historically, directors have used white actors and actresses to play Asians, but today one of the big issues in the entertainment industry is the casting of ethnic roles.

_____

_____

○ *Dances with Wolves* was named best picture of 1990.

_____

_____

○ By the year 2000, about 5 percent of the total U.S. population will be Asian American.

_____

_____

○ Asian American actors and actresses should have the opportunity to play Asian roles in movies and the theater.

_____

_____

B. Do you agree or disagree with the writer's position as stated in the essay? Why? Write a summary statement that expresses your own position on the casting of ethnic roles.

_____

_____

_____

_____

_____

Book Test

PART 1: FICTION

Read the following scene from a play. Underline and draw circles to show relationships between words and ideas. Make notes in the margins as you read. Then use the selection and your notes to answer the questions on the next page.

CHARACTERS: TONY: a 14-year-old boy who is about to leave his pueblo to go to high school in a large city

ROXANNE: a 14-year-old girl from the same pueblo

SETTING: The shade of a large cottonwood tree. The tree is located along a river that runs through the pueblo in New Mexico. It is early fall, and the leaves on the tree are just beginning to turn a lovely golden color.

1   TONY: (*Gazing at river*) I can't believe we'll be in Santa Fe next week! What do you think school will be like?

3   ROXANNE: I don't know. It will be exciting, I'm sure. But also scary! (*She grimaces slightly.*) I'm not sure I'll feel comfortable living outside the pueblo. I mean, I'll miss my family during the week. I keep wondering what the city students will be like. Will I fit in?

8   TONY: (*Turning to* ROXANNE) I know what you mean. Sometimes I feel so secure. Our people have lived here for so many years. Each rock, each tree is special! Still, I long to go to a bigger school. (*He smiles gently at* ROXANNE *and then says hesitating,*) What if . . . the students don't understand our ways? Will we have to give up much of what we're used to?

14   ROXANNE: Maybe we should stay right here.

15   TONY: My family would never accept that decision. I know I would not be content either. (*He sighs.*)

16   ROXANNE: (*Touching* TONY's *hand gently*) Either way, where do we belong?

A. Use the selection and your notes to identify the best answer to each question.

1. Which meaning of the word *secure* is used in line 9 of this play?

    a. to pledge payment
    b. free from risks
    c. to guarantee
    d. to tie up

2. The words in this scene that BEST reflect the writer's message are

    a. *I know what you mean.*
    b. *Will I fit in?*
    c. *Where do we belong?*
    d. *I feel so secure.*

3. What is the most probable outcome of this scene?

    a. Tony and Roxanne marry.
    b. Only Tony goes to the school
    c. Only Roxanne goes to the school.
    d. Roxanne and Tony both go to the school.

4. To whom is Roxanne referring when she uses the pronoun *we* in line 14?

    a. herself and Tony
    b. all the Pueblo people
    c. herself and her family
    d. all students at school

5. Tony and Roxanne feel insecure about leaving the pueblo. This best describes

    a. the plot.
    b. the action.
    c. the resolution.
    d. the conflict.

6. Roxanne suggests that they should stay in the pueblo

    a. after Tony wonders if they will fit in.
    b. when Tony gazes at the river.
    c. after Roxanne touches Tony's hand.
    d. after Tony wonders about giving up what they are used to.

B. Imagine Tony and Roxanne at the high school in Sante Fe. Write two or three sentences to describe an important problem they might face there and the way in which they might solve it.

_____

_____

_____

_____

_____

_____

_____

_____

_____

Book Test

PART 2: NONFICTION

Read the editorial below. Circle words and write notes in the margins as you ask yourself questions. Then use the selection and your notes to answer the questions on the next page.

Extend the Ban on Smoking

1 With increasing frequency, more and more individuals, businesses, and even whole towns have decided that cigarette smoking is not for them. But what about you? Would you support a nationwide ban on smoking in public places? We applaud the smoke-free workplace, the nonsmoking restaurant, and the absence of smoke-filled air on planes. It is time to accept and extend the ban on public smoking.

2 Scientific research has shown that cigarette smoking is dangerous to the health of the smoker and the nonsmoker. Studies have shown that it is the leading cause of lung cancer, emphysema, and chronic asthma in the United States today. Furthermore, it can cause harm to the development of a fetus, tends to aggravate high blood pressure, and increases harmful cholesterol levels. It is also an addictive, dirty, and very expensive habit.

3 By giving smokers the right to smoke in public places, we are taking away the right of others to enjoy clean, smoke-free air. Our children are especially at risk. By allowing smoking in public places, we are taking away their right to breathe clean, smoke-free air. We are also sending them the wrong message. The message is that cigarette smoking is neither harmful nor offensive.

4 Smoke from cigarettes is also a deadly pollutant. Recent studies have shown the dangers of breathing secondary smoke, which is the smoke inhaled by a nonsmoker. The results from these studies show that an alarming number of lung cancer deaths occurred among people who lived with smokers but did not smoke themselves.

5 Given the evidence, do you believe that nonsmokers should be protected from the deadly effects of cigarette smoke? If you do, help support the effort to extend the ban on public smoking. We'll all be healthier for it.

A. Use the selection and your notes to identify the best answer or answers to each question.

1. With which statement below would the writer of this editorial agree?

    a. We must all try to treat smokers more fairly.

    b. Smokers should not have their rights taken away.

    c. Smokers deserve no consideration at all.

    d. Smokers' rights are secondary to health.

2. Which of the following are key words related directly to the subject?

    a. *secondary smoke*

    b. *smoke-free workplace*

    c. *studies* and *research*

    d. *dangerous*

3. How would you describe the sentences in paragraph 3?

    a. mostly facts

    b. mostly opinion

    c. all facts

    d. all opinions

4. Which words give clues to the meaning of *ban* in the title and in paragraph 1?

    a. *smoke-free*

    b. *nonsmoking*

    c. *absence*

    d. *frequency*

5. According to the editorial, what are the results of NOT extending the smoking ban?

    a. more polluted air

    b. more lung cancer, emphysema, and high blood pressure

    c. loss of nonsmokers' rights

    d. loss of smokers' rights

6. Which persuasive technique does the last sentence in paragraph 2 illustrate?

    a. facts that appeal to reason

    b. storytelling to make a point

    c. statistics supporting the topic

    d. an opinion that appeals to emotion

B. Write a brief summary of the editorial. At the end of your summary, tell whether or not you think the writer's persuasive techniques were effective. Use examples to support your response.

_____

_____

_____

_____

_____

_____

_____

_____

_____

_____